RETAIL BUSINESS MANAGEMENT

Theory and Principles

RETAIL BUSINESS MANAGEMENT

Theory and Principles

Yoginder Singh

2008

CYBER TECH PUBLICATIONS
4264/3 Ansari Road, Daryaganj, New Delhi - 110 002

Retail Business Management

First Edition 2008

Published by G.S. Rawat

For Cyber Tech Publications

4264/3, Ansari Road, Daryaganj, New Delhi - 110 002

E-mail : cyberpublicationsdelhi@yahoo.com

Phone : 011-23244078,

Fax : 011-23280028

Printed at

Amit Enterprises, Moujpur, Delhi. Ph. - 9810878184

Preface

Modern Retail is making an assault on India. Over the next few years we are likely to see the most impressive success stories within the worldwide retail industry. We are undoubtedly going to see dramatic failure as well. The opportunity that is represented by the current minimal penetration of so-called 'organised' retail has created a whirlwing of enthusiasm that the world has perhaps not seen.

Certainly there is no-where else were we have seen a headlong rush into retail by conglomerates with no previous experience in the industry. The investments quoted by our largest new players are unprecedented. It may even seem bizarre to the outside world that the highest level of monetary investment in India is pouring into a sector that is not even recognized as an industry.

My publisher and his staffmembers have assisted in every possible ways and have worked hard for its timely completion of this deserve and readers patronage.

—Editor

Contents

1

Principles of Retail Sales Management

Retailing is a set of activities performed in selling the goods and services directly to the end users. The goods and services sold to the consumers are meant for their personal use and not for resale or business activity. Retailing is the last activity conducted in the chain of product distribution down to the consumers. In principle, retailing is a business activity which involves the sale of goods and services to a large number of consumers spread in a large area. The retailer or a retail store is like any business enterprise whose sales volume comes primarily from retailing. There are different forms of retailing. Many of the forms keep emerging according to the convenience of the buyers and retailers. In large towns, retailing is organized and mostly performed through stores and automatic vending machines.

However, in the rural areas, the retailing of goods and services are conducted through a traditional pattern by displaying the goods in mobile vans, carts and on footpaths. For understanding the types of retailers and their functions, we can broadly classify the retailing network into two categories—(i) store retailing and (ii) non-store retailing. Like the growth cycle of business firms, the retailing activity also passes through the stages of embrayonic, growth, maturity and decline. A retail store observes the period of accelerated growth, reaches the stage of maturity and starts declining. It has been observed that the retail stores of older fashion took more than five decades to reach the stage of maturity in terms of the volume of sales. However, in the modern era, the store retail types reach their maturity very fast due to the organized retailing management. Some of the major store retailers are briefly descried here:

- Department store
- Exclusive retail store or speciality store
- Supermarkets
- Convenience store
- Superstore, hyper markets
- Discount store Non-franchise or catalog store

Department Store

A department store offers a wide range of products in an organized fashion and is easily accessible to the consumers. The product-line of the department stores are substantially long. The department stores provide better amenities to the consumers for shopping by developing adequate infrastructure for parking, leisure and hobbies. The department stores face a close competition from the discount shops and down-town retailers of poor quality goods. The department stores provide consumer services of honouring the product guarantee, warranty, post-sale services and the latest technical information. The department stores also organize educational programmes for the benefit of consumer on the various aspects of product use and related matters.

Exclusive or speciality retail stores unlike department stores donot carry along product-line. These stores are narrow in product-line and are largely confined to the product-line of a specific company. Thus, they present a deep assortment within that product-line. Examples can be drawn from many consumer goods companies promoting exclusive retail stores like Phillips for a range of electrical, audio and video household gadgets; Raymods for textiles; Bata for shoes and leather goods and so on.

The exclusive stores can also be further classified as:

- Single line stores
- Limited line stores
- Super speciality stores

The single line stores may be identified as the retail stores selling only one product like textiles. The limited line stores maybe defined as the shops having micro specialization, based on the goods and services, gender and age like exclusive Men's Wear retail stores, Kid's Shoppe for garments etc. The retail stores engaged in selling products scientifically designed for a particular purpose may be categorized as super speciality stores e.g. surgical equipments stores, sports accessories, fashion garments stores and the like. The classification of retail stores and their functions may be well understood through the retail position map plotted.

Supermarkets

Supermarkets are also a type of organized retail stores which handle relatively a large volume of goods and services at a low cost—high margin principle of retailing. The consumers are provided franchise in the super markets and are largely organized as self-service outlets. The supermarkets exhibit a long range of product-line of various consumer needs like grocery, household appliances, entertainment. Toys, garments etc. it has been observed that supermarkets earn an operating profit of 1-2 percent on their sales and 10-15 per cent on their net worth. The supermarkets also provide consumer conveniences like in-shop entertainment, pantry, home delivery service, opinion survey and consumer education. The supermarkets have chain retailing in many countries like Woolworth in UK and Europe.

There is a marginal difference between the super-stores

and hyper-stores. The latter category of stores operates in a larger area (approximately 1-2 lakh square feet) wide range of products. These markets have a combination of all retail functions like credit services, discounts, finance and related services. The basic approach of hyper stores is exhibiting a wide range of assorted products for all type of consumers and displaying them in bulk. The product handling costs in such stores would be minimum and they also function as sole distributors to the convenience stores.

Convenience Stores

There stores are of small retail outlets located near the residential areas for the convenience of the consumers. They are open for long hours all through the week. This category of stores carry al limited line of consumer products. The convenience stores operate at a high turnover and relative higher profit basis as compared to any of the other retail stores. The consumers seem to be willing to pay a higher price to the retailers for the convenience provided to them at their door steps.

Discount Stores

In principle, a discount store should sell all types of merchandise offering largely reputed brands at lower prices but not inferior goods. In the recent days, some of the consumer products manufacturing companies own discount retail stores to sell their second grade products as earmarked by their quality control division. Hence, the discount retail stores have moved from general stores down to speciality merchandise stores such as discount sporting goods stores, garments, shoes, electronic books and the like.

Catalog Showroom the catalog stores is a new generation super stores which deal with a variety of goods and services of wide range. Such stores conduct retailing operation of all types of goods including interiors, construction material, mechanical gadgets, electronics, and many more. The consumers buying goods from catalog shops have to indent for the specific goods as per the inventory specification in the catalog, the consumers wait in the designated place for the delivery of goods and sometimes, the stores arrange home delivery of heavy products. The catalog stores provide a return facility to the consumers within a stipulated period. The goods can be returned to the stores, if the consumers are not satisfied.

Non-store Retailing

Besides the on-store retailing, the direct selling approaches have emerged in the recent past as an effective sales instrument. The direct selling is one of the popular non-store retailing activity, largely for the consumer goods. The sales representatives of the company/distributor canvas the product on a door to door basis and contribute in augmenting the sales. The automatic vending machines for selling some of the consumer products like chilled beverages etc., are also of non-store retailing approaches. The specific non-store retailing types are:

- Direct Marketing
- Automatic Vending Machines
- Business by mail Order
- Tele-shopping or Net-shopping
- Mobile Retailing

The multi-level retailing stores, chain retailing stores, cooperatives network and merchandise conglomerate are the new forms of retailing that have emerged in the recent past.

Decision-making in Retailing

Retailing is considered as one of the scientific grassroots level selling approaches in the modern era. Hence, a retailer has to make the right decision at the right time to promote his retail business. The specific areas which needs to be planned properly are (i) choice of place (i) choice of products—assorted or exclusive (iii) price level (iv) tools of retailing and (v) consumer services. The decision regarding the choice of place and products are inter-related e.g. in the high income locality, a retailer should plan for high price assorted product stores vis-à-vis in low income consumer locality.

Tools of Retailing

Retailing is an art. The retail stores playa vital role in the product promotion as they are directly associated with the consumers. A successful retailer tries to get the consumers involved in the trade by providing a goods reception, facilities and respect to them. However a retailer follows a variety of approaches to make his retailing a success. Some of the tools used by he retailers for promoting their business are listed below:

(i) The retailers dealing with similar products form an association to carry out jointly the promotion activities kike advertising, pricing and other related matters.

(ii) The retailers do pre-ticketing by placing price tags on the products indicating all the required information of the product like, date of manufacturing, size, volume, name of the manufacturer, date of expiry, product code of the manufacturer as well as retailer for any complaints of reordering.

(iii) The retailer also help the consumers in re-indenting the products by sending them reminders and catalog of the products by sending them reminders, and catalog of the products.

(iv) The retailers also introduces special prices during the peak seasons for a storewide promotion.

(v) The consumers enjoy the privilege of returning or exchanging the damaged goods without paying any additional price.

(vi) The distributors and company representatives get the sponsorship of the retailer for demonstrating their products in the stores.

Besides these services, the retail stores provide many pre-and post-purchase services to satisfy the consumers. The pre-purchase services include, accepting an order on telephone and by mail, in-store and outside the store advertising , interior and window display, consumer conveniences, fitting rooms, shopping hours, organising consumer entertainment like integrated cable TV, fashion shows, recipe contest, baby shows etc. The retailers provide selected post-purchase services to the consumers such as home delivery of goods, gift packaging, returns and exchanges, tailoring, installations, demonstrations, accepting credit transactions and cheques. In addition to the listed services large and chain retail stores provide leisure and general amenities to the consumers like rest rooms for consumers, baby sittings, restaurants etc.

Wholesaling

Wholesaling is an activity which supplies the goods and services to the agencies for reselling. In other words, wholesaling includes all such activities involved in selling the goods and services to the retailers or any intermediate channel between the consumer and wholesaler. They perform key functions in selling the goods and services to the retailers. The major functions of the wholesalers are:

- Sales and product promotion
- Counseling retailers of or assortment building
- Bulk breaking and small packaging
- Transportation
- Warehousing
- Financing
- Risk bearing
- Providing market Information.

The wholesalers on one hand supply the finished goods and services to the retailers and on the other also engage themselves in procuring raw products for the processors. Thus, it can be stated that a large category of wholesalers play a dual role in procurement and distribution.

The various types of wholesalers may be classified as under

- Exclusive wholesale distributors
- Wholesale procurement and distributors
- Industrial distributors
- Mail-order wholesalers
- Commission agents.

Concept of Sales

Selling is an àrt largely associated with the behavioural skills of the sales personnel of a sales organisation in recent days, selling is performed using scientific methods of product presentation, advertising and various approaches drawn to take the consumer into confidence. The efficiency of sales depends on the type of sales person and the techniques utilized in selling goods or services. The consumers are the decision-makers in buying the goods and services proposed for sales and hence play the key role in eh process of sales. There are four distinguished categories of sales which include each type of sales position. These types of selling are:

- Consultative a sales
- Technical sales
- Commercial sales
- Direct sales

These categories require a specific management approach for conducting the task in the market. The details of management approaches are discussed in the foregoing text.

Consultative Sales

Consultative sales may be defined as an approach of

selling specific goods or services to the technical organisations. The consultative type of companies keep the accounts of their clients and assign the sales force to attend and the specific client accounts. Examples of computer systems management, structural planning of factories, human resource management, capital market services and the like may be listed in the category of consultative sales. Since performing sales for the goods and services of this category involves high skills, they require low-key, low-pressure approach for the sales personnel. It requires a comprehensive knowledge of the product or services and the user orientative. A successful salesperson in this field needs to have strong confidence and an experience of few larger successes achieved periodically. Of all the sales types the consultative sales is probably the most professional and demands the highest compensation for the skills and abilities of the salespersons.

Technical Sales

The product knowledge, its application, relevance to contemporary technology development and sales skills are the essential characteristics that need to be present in the salespeople engaged in the sales of goods and services of technical products. The dominant industries in this field are electronics, engineering products of all branches, medical equipments and the like the buying influence is generally drawn from a professional manger. The personal sales in this category is limited. However, the organisational sales of technical goods and services are higher as compared to personal sales. The compensation to he sales force of this category is of the lined with performance besides a low salary.

Commercial Sales and Direct Sales

A large sales force is engaged in performing the commercial sales of goods and services of consumption nature. These sales are very much individual consumer oriented. The sales personnel operate as sales representatives of the company or as facilitators of an in-house retail stores, the major takeoff of the sales representatives will be to collect orders from the consumers or organisations. Informing the direct sales, the representatives attempt to generate an emotional appeal and motivate the buyer. It has been observed that the turnover rate in the direct sales is higher as compared to the other three categories of sales. The sales personnel engaged in direct sales require a strong persuasive ability and skills to identify a prospects' buying motives. The direct salespeople receive the compensation in terms of commission on the volume of sales.

Organising Sales Force

Sales force can be organized in many ways, subject to the product type, coverage and buyers, prospects. The different ways of organising the sales force are:

- Region-based sales force (territorial)
- Product-based
- Market-based

The region-based sales forces may be organized for the vertical and horizontal coverage of different areas spread across the operational area, horizontal overage of different areas spread across the operational area. The vertical hierarchy of the sales force may be cent al-level, zonal-level, area-level and down to the markets located in the various towns. The horizontal area of operation may be in a given area across the towns or villages. The size of the sales force depends on the geographical spread, volume of sales and density of buyers.

The product-based sales force generally belongs to a company and functions as a team to promote the sales of the product in the given area. Example may be cited of any automobile company. The sales force needs to be distrinctly organized for the product in tune with the functional requirements of the market. Example may be cited of the service marketing for the computer industries product in the market. To market such service, a group of professional sales and service engineers are required to boost up the market of principle product as well the service packages of the ancillary unit. The major steps for effective selling in any category of sales organisation are listed below:

Prospecting and qualifying: Collecting basic information about consumers, references, joining prospect's organisation, initiating communication.

Negotiation about the orders, delivery, pre and post-sales service, organisational benefits and the like.

Approach: The sales package.

Presentation and demonstration Convincing the buyer.

Problem solving Resolving conflicts pertaining to all P's and A's.

Delivering Closing the deal by satisfying the consumer.

Follow-up Post-sales service and maintaining relationship.

Sales Management and Control

The sales executives or managers play a significant role in the performance of sales in terms of volume, net profit and long term growth. This requires coordination involving organisation, planning and marketing strategy. The coordination for getting a higher sales order requires minimizing the cross work handled by the different departments in an organisation. The decision-making process should be streamlinged and participatory approaches should be encouraged in designing the right sales strategies.

The sales executives should plan the sales targets and approaches according to the marketing objectives of the company. The draft sales plans should be prepared and appraised to achieve the desired results at an optimum cost. The sales executive as a member of the business planning group shodldevelp such a market plan that is approapriat formarket conditions and reflect the probable cntribution of the saesforce.

Tehsales executives shoudlalso coordinate with the distribution network andmanage rth supply of goods and services on the given time schedule, He has to coordinate the personal selling with the marketing efforts of the carrying and forwarding (C&F) agents and wholesale dealers (WD) The following aspects of coordination are important for the sales executive for the effective distribution of goods and services.

- Gaining product distribution
- Getting dealer identification
- Reconciling business goals
- Sharing promotional risks.

Gaining the product distribution is a high task for the sales executives in case of the new products, unless the trade margins are competitive and the package of deal includes some incentives. The C&F agents and WDs refuse to accept the distribution of the new products on various economic and physical grounds. The sales executives should playa crucial role in convincing the distributors. Some of the manufacturers go for forced distribution through heavy advertisement and consumer pull strategies. The sales executive should ensure that the consumers know the outlets, dealers, stockist and agents of the goods and services, the access to outlets and the layout are important issues to be considered in promotion of the sales volume. In adeute dealer identification results in clogged distribution channels right from the dealer network to the factory. Many times the conflicts are developed in the distribution of the goods and services due to rivalry and brand hoax. This situation needs to be handled skillfully by the sales executives through an effective distributor coordination. The less the manufacturer and the distributors work at cross purposes, the greater the return to both the parties. The information management from the market to the manufacturer and vice versa is an important task in coordinating the sales. The sales executives have to make periodical appraisal of the existing marketing policies in reference to the marketing information made available by the distributors. There are different strategies for ensuring effective sales management. Some of them are setting quantitative performance standards, factual analysis of market information, comparing results and standards and sales variation adjustment approaches.

The quantitative standards are set for the product sales after careful analysis of SWOT to measure the performance of the product sales. The process of standard setting requires continuous experimentation and consumer behaviour analysis. The standard setting requires the identification of a dynamic work force. Such standards are set in ranges indicating acceptable performance. The a market information system need to be strengthened ensuring the factual information flow to help decision-making insetting the performance standards. Besides, the sales functions may be controlled through the informal and formal approaches. The large organisations need written sales policies for uniform implementation of the strategies. The sales policies should be formulated from the through review of the tangible information. The sales control standards can also be developed on the basis of fixing the target estimating the anticipated sales of the product in the market. Sales volume performance is best appraised by comparing it with potential sales volume or the targets. The formal control is required as of or sales budgetary controls and setting up the sales territories. The budgetary control mechanisms help control over the margins and expenditure and so over the profit. Hence, the sales management is a challenging task and assigns broad responsibilities.

Principles of Selling

Selling is a creative action and has to be performed according to the needs of the buyers, distributors and the market in total. The most popular principle of sales is AIDAS—attention, interest, desire, action and satisfaction. It has been observed that training programmes on sales management largely focus on this principle, as it is directly associated with the buyer behaviour. It is necessary for the sales person to first set the buyer's receptive state of mind and secure his attention. It is generally carried out by opening up a good conversation to relax the buyer and gradually set the information on the goods and services. Generally, it is advantageous. If the opening remarks are about the prospect (buyer) and favouring the business. The second goal is to intensify the prospect's interests is largely affected by the learning and motivation process. The third stage of this principle is to prompt the desire of the prospect to buy the goods and services of the company. In this process, it is required for the sales person to keep the conversation effective and continuous till the prospect makes up his mind towards buying the goods and services of the company. At the end of the favourable conversation with the prospect, the sales person should induce the buying process by getting the purchase order signed and look into the other formalities required for delivering the goods and services of the company. However, buying is not a spontaneous action and as a behaviour it has to be induced. The prospect has to be given a chance for trial of the goods and services and other incentives to make his decision final. Lastly, the AIDAS principle advocates to build up the level of satisfaction of the prospect and it has to be reassured by the company or the sales person that the buying decision was correct.

The Situation Response Theory of Selling explains the concept that everything was right for that sales." Such sales happen in the fairs, exhibitions and buyers' crowd and these are mutually induced by the buyers themselves. Some of the proponents of this theory feel that the selling appeals evoke the desired responses in the buyers. This is a seller oriented principle and largely induced by the external factors like friend's appeal, impulse buying, me-too behaviour of the buyers and buying advantages and incentives.

The principle of the Buying Formula is prospect-oriented and emphasizes the buyer's side of the buyer-seller relationship. According to this principle the buyer's need receives the prime attention and the role of the sales persons is to help the buyer to find the best possible solution. This process passes through the four stages which include (i) need of problem of the buyer (ii) possible solution (iii) purchase decision and (iv) getting satisfaction. The purchase decision involves many external variable like brand, quality, purchase options, word of mouth insights, price, post-sales services, status etc., which play a significant role in inducing the buyer behaviour.

The Behavioural Equation principle of selling is based on the theory of situation response. It is an advanced version and more behaviour orientated explaining the drive, cue, response and reinforcement. The drives are stronger stimuli attached to influence the buyer's response. There are two types of drives that influence the purchase behaviour—(i) innate drives or basic needs or problems and (ii) learned drives such as social approval, status, high perceived use value and the like. On the contrary, cues are the weak stimuli which appear from different types of decision inputs—(i) triggering cues which activate the decision process the given goods and services. (i) non-triggering cues do not activate the purchase behaviour but they do influence the decision-making process, and (iii) information cues support the triggering cues to helping decision-making and purchase behaviour process. The response factor is what the buyer ultimately acts upon and reinforcement is any even that strengthens the buyer's tendency to make a particular response.

The Importance of Convenience in Consumer Purchasing

Both product and convenience costs influence consumer purchasing behaviour. The increased importance consumers are attaching to convenience offers a key to understanding consumer shopping behaviour and is a major opportunity for markets. Consumer valuation of several forms of convenience is discussed, with special attention devoted to place convenience.

Two factor are of utmost importance in understanding consumer shopping behaviour. First, consumers making shopping decisions achieve an equilibrium between commodity costs and convenience costs. Second, convenience costs are assuming more importance as patronage determinants.

Commodity costs are defined as the monetary price paid the seller to obtain possession of goods and services. Convenience costs are incurred through the expenditure of time, physical and nervous energy, and money required to overcome the frictions of space and time, and to obtain succession of goods and services. For instance, a consumer shopping in the business district spends time, energy, and frequently carfare or working fees, in addition to commodity expenditures. Such costs have always been involved in trading decisions. The new emphasis on conscience does not necessarily mean that consumers are less price conscious formerly, rather, insistence on convenience cost minimization has been superimposed on the desire for economically favourable commodity transactions.

Shopping Costs

The question of consumer time expenditures for shopping is an interesting one. t has been estimated that there is a minimum of five billion adult leisure hours each week in the United States. This reflects is part a population consensus to accept a substantial share of the benefits of the production and marketing revolutions in increased leisure. Paradoxically, the increase in leisure time has been accompanied by a reaction against spending much of that leisure shopping. The modern family is confronted with too many more attractive possible uses of time.

Many forces favour higher consumer valuations of leisure and other convenience considerations. The suburban population movement with is living habit changes and broader family interests is one such force s urban areas also, fundamental social forces are operating which has resulted in families functioning more as a group than as individuals is certain activities, even to the extent of buying together. Such force favouring higher convenience cost valuations include the large numbers of working housewives, the age group imbalance within the population, and higher educational levels. Consumer estimates of purchasing costs are determined by the evaluations of alternative trading and social opportunities. Purchase decisions are made at the point whether total of commodity and convenience costs are considered minimal.

On the supply side sellers are operating in what seems to be a increasingly standardized production and legal matrix which is tending as limit price competition. The relatively narrow price spread among most retailers carrying identical nationally advertised merchandise suggests new importance for convenience costs in the strategy determination sellers. It appears reasonable to speculate that the range of competition advantage based on commodity costs will narrow. In this setting, it probable that convenience considerations will assume more importance determinants of purchase behaviour and seller strategy, and that more the competition of the future will focus on convenience considerations will assume more importance determinants of purchase behaviour and seller strategy, and that more the competition of the future will focus on convenience consideration.

Ten Convenience Forms

The importance of convenience as a determinant of consumer acceptance of products and services can be observed in an increasingly range of convenience features built into new products and in new convenience form appearing in the marketing system. Charles G. Mortine President of the General Foods Corporation, has described ten forms convenience which the American consumer now expects almost as a matter of course.

(i) *Form Convenience*—cigarettes in various sizes and tips, and vet-pocket radios.

(ii) *Time Convenience*—typified by evening hours, and fresh fruits and vegetables out of season.

(iii) *Place Convenience*—file insurance in airline terminals, drive-it-yourself automobile rental services; and the planned shopping center.

(iv) *Quantity or Unit convenience*—aspirin in tins of 12, or bottles of 500; an small pianos for the smaller home.

(v) *Packaging convenience*—disposable and utility packages; and the packaged vacation plan. The packaged home is already on the market.

(vi) *Readiness convenience*—instant coffee; pre-cooked foods; and The Reader's Digest.

(vii) *Combination Convenience*—do it yourself kits; and combination and matched sets.

(viii) *Automatic Operations Convenience*—automatic kitchen equipment; power steering and brakes on automobiles; and automation in many fields

(ix) *Selection Convenience*—the new variety of dairy products; and automobile color combinations.

(x) *Credit Convenience-cars*; homes; vacation cruises; and education on credit.

Four Aspects of Place Convenience

Sellers should study all ten convenience forms to find areas in which consumer convenience costs may be reduced. This article is concerned specifically with place convenience. In maximizing place convenience advantages, sellers have related decisions at for levels to make about the capital positions that products ideally should occupy in the market.

(1) The geographic area or areas in which the goods or services are to be offered must be selected. In these areas or markets are found the consumers of the goods. This seller decision usually is not of concerned to the shopper who may choose from the offering of many sellers of substitute products.

The shopping mobility of consumers has tended to be limited to one metropolitan area, but this may not be the case in the future. Perhaps larger scale retailers may become concerned about competition between metropolitan areas as well as with competition within a metropolitan area. For instance, it may represent the same expenditure of convenience costs for a West Hartford resident to order by mail from Hartford, r even to make the trip to downtown Hartford. Conceivably, Hartford department store could become concerned about the drawing power of New York, Boston, and Providence department stores, as well as competition form suburban Hartford stores.

On the other hand, as metropolitan areas grow together to form urban regions, the primate cities of New York, Chicago, and Los Angeles are likely to lose some of their retail leadership to burgeoning regional and provincial metropolitan areas. This may occur in the same fashion, and for much the same reasons; that the central business district has lost ground to suburban elements in the retail structure.

(2) The most satisfactory positions within the market must be selected from those offered by distributors and retailers selling space in the market Channel-of-distribution decisions are involved. The one-stop shopping tendency of consumers has made channel selection more difficult for sellers in today's fluid market.

(3) Choices must be made among competing retail and wholesale institutions offering access to the customer. Should a full service hole sale be utilized, or would a limited function wholesaler represent a better channel choice? Are urban or suburban positions preferred? What is the role of the shopping centre?

The planned shopping centre movement can be rationalized with some justification in terms of consumer convenience. At the same time, planned centers are more than devices for convenient shopping or mechanisms for retail sales expansion in suburban areas. Planned shopping centers are a basic part of the restructuring of metropolitan communities. Their long-term importance to the economy is based on a continuing reassessment in consumers of shopping and social activities. Consumer convenience is still probably the basis of the shopping center movement. But the social economic, and architectural concepts underlyıng planned centers as geared to a new kind of social pattern and to what maybe an eruption into a new American social dimension in which consumer desires still require new patterns of marketing.

(4) Problems of positioning of goods within outlets must be settled Display and layout decisions are involved at this level. An experiment by Alfred Politiz Suggests the importance of convenience within the store studying the anatomy of the sale, he purchased and operated a large hardware store in Tampa, Florida. He found that if a product is sufficient well known to get consumer acceptance and is conveniently location the consumer will buy it in preference to a better known product. Why the customer will not select a product he has not heard about, "the little bit of inconvenience wipes out the impressiveness of even the known brands."

Conflicting Cost Considerations

A dominant characteristic of consumer goods marketing at present the state of flux of consumer valuations of commodity and conveniences costs. While such developments as the discount house reflect strong consumer interest in the reduction of commodity costs, it is quite possible that convenience costs will increase in importance as patronage determinants for more low dollar value items. This will pose anew one of the most challenging problems facing retailers in our complex distribution system: offering the right mix of convenience and economy to customers. Rich rewards may go to merchants able to do this successfully. A wedding of the shopping center concept and the discount house idea represents one promising approach.

Convenience cost pressures are likely to affect more marketing agencies in the future. Some of the possible impacts on planned shopping centers an established business districts are suggested below.

Convenience forces and the Retail structure

Planned Center Increase

The shopping center movement is so new that currently two-thirds of existing centers are less than five years old. This fact, together with the predicted center expansion, indicated that the full impact of the movement has yet to be felt. A fundamental change in the retail structure of metropolitan communities seems certain, as a result of shopping center growth. Over 10,000 planned shopping centers are now in operation. Estimates have been made that by 1975, 17,500 of them will be operating. This means a planned shopping center for each 14,000 of a projected 1975 population of 245 million. This expansion is not expected to be uninterrupted. Many poorly planned intermediate centers are particularly velnerable to new competition.

Individual stores and shopping centers are tending to be larger. Department store branches of 300,000 square feet, and super markets of 50,000square feet have already appeared. A minimum site for regional centers seed to be considered fifty acres. Regional center developers are now thinking in terms of one hundred acres as a minimum site. Tracts of this extremely expensive, especially if they are in or near large cities. The increasing size of regional centers may mean that in the future such centers will be located farther from large population concentrations, and center the suburban periphery.

Consumer convenience considerations also set a limit to the growth of individual stores and centers. For instance, it is generally agreed that shoppers resist walking more than 600 feet from their parked cars to the latest center store. With planned centers, this suggests a limit for the maximum-parking distance that can be used before the planned center its advantages over unplanned shopping districts.

The Distance Concept and Convenience

The distance concept involves time-cost elements rather than a purely special one. High speed roads enabling consumers to travel farther from home on shopping trips are changing consumer views on distance. IN our society of automobile-borne suburbanites, distance between metropolitans point swill increasingly be judged on a time basis, not a mileage basis. The impact of this on established retail patterns is already evident. Downtown retailers have had to compete aggressively for suburban business is order to hold a satisfactory market position. Effective downtown competition for suburban trade is still possible. Indeed, a pattern for the rehabilitation of central business districts has developed. It includes improving access traffic, and parking conditions; modernizing physical facilities; conducting imaginative promotions; and strengthening mass transportation. In short, it means restoring some of the lost convenience aspects to center business district shopping.

Changing Functions in the Metropolitan Retail Structure

The central business district and suburban shopping center provide essential but different services to the community. Retail functions within the central business district and the other elements of the metropolitan retail structure are being modified. Store locations are shifting in the inner core, inner belt, and outer belt of the central business district and miss business thoroughfares. Similarly, retailers in planned an unplanned secondary commercial sub-districts, neighborhood business streets, small store clusters, and planned regional shopping centers are modifying functions to adapt to the needs of consumers living and shopping overall wide area. The downtown are may respond by becoming more of a business service, and recreational center and less of a mercantile one opinions as this vary widely. Frank Lloyd Wright visualizes the city of the future without a central shopping district. Others anticipate a downtown stimulated in part by shopping center competition, which will furthermore downtown property owners and merchants into rehabilitation and redesign programmes.

Other Dimensions of Convenience

In addition to spatial and temporal aspects, convenience has social and esthetic dimensions. This is one reason shopping center are likely to play an increasingly important role in community social life. All shopping centers are likely to benefit by following a policy of community identification although the benefits are particularly apparent with the large community and regional centers. Auditoriums, meeting rooms, restaurants, and other facilities making shopping more convenient are found in more planned centers. As more planned centers include such amenity shopping centers may come to resemble earlier market places, which served social as well as trading functions.

Consumers favour centers in which merchandise is presented conveniently, informally, and interestingly. Shopping-center planning, therefore, the excitement and pleasure to shopping. The modified bazaar concept of the center is likely to gain favour as weather-controlled centers without window displays and partitions come into being. For instance, Southdale, the new regional center outside Minneapolis, has a glass enclosed mall connecting the various stores in the center.

Convenience and New Retail Types

New store types are likely to appear in planned centers. Since shopping centers are located on choice, relatively low cost land compared to downtown stores, one floor retailing operations are possible to an extent not practical downtown. This may mean a reduction in handling costs and in the number of people needed to conduct and supervise operations. Some specialty store in planned centers should be in a position to offer more variety in prices and styles than down town specialty stores operating in less space.

Convenience pressures may provide a stimulus for other retailing developments offering lower convenience costs to consumers. Among these maybe increased direct-to-consumer selling, catalogue and telephone willing, perhaps a combination of television and telephone selling, and automatic vending machines. Improved vending equipment selling an increasing broad variety of merchandise could turn some planned centers and store clusters into round-the-clock merchandising machines.

Metropolitan for Decision Making

Understanding of the current state of the art requires acceptance of change itself as the dominant characteristic of marketing. If understanding of the process of market change, the forces producing change, and therefore, ability to develop policies under accelerated change condition is to be increased, more attention to the convenience aspects of marketing seems justified.

Measurement of convenience costs, while difficult, is not impossible Reillys Law represents one approach to quantifying some convenience dynamics, which beganin1927, that retail business gravitated from smaller cities and towns in accordance with a definite law. Reilly based has law of retail gravitation on two rules. The first is that, the larger the city the more outside trade it will draw. The second rule is that a city draw more trade from nearby towns than distant ones.

Reilly's contribution was in providing a quantitative measure of the rate that trade increases as the population of a city increases. His law of retail gravitation follows: Two cities attract retail trade from any intermediate city or town in the vicinity of the breaking point approximately in direct proportion to the population of the two cities and in inverse proportion to the square of the distances (via most direct in proved automobile highway) from these two cities to the intermediate town.

The law can be supplemented by discounts based on surveys, observations to obtain approximations of convenience cost consideration in trade areas. Factors such as time expenditures, distance (including distance to the store and with the store), and intervening shopping opportunities can be isolated in individual experiments. Development of consumer-distance concept to measure the costs of various locations possible. This could be based on the number of consumers within an multiples by driving time minutes from a location.

But the core convenient analysis lies in the area of consumer psychology and sociology. This means that marketers will have to absorb more of what the and other disciplines, in addition to economics, have to contribute marketing theory.

Market Segmentation and Consumer Behaviour

In addition to the number of consumers and their incomes, the distribution of consumers over space is important to marketers. Changes in population distribution are producing important economic social, and marketing consequences. Interurbia is defined as "as agglomeration of cities and surrounding, densely populated, non farm counties," Marketers have a vital interests in the commercial impact of interurbia, and in the problems and opportunities created by this new population distribution pattern. Interurbian psychology and advertising media factors are discussed.

Interurbia: The Changing Face of America

Background

As a nation, we did not reckon with the pace of our growth. The quickened pace of our population growth has caused the Census Bureau to increase its forecast for 1965 by four million...its 1976 forecast by over 7 million.

The dimensions of the automobile boom were not foreseen either. In 1953, hard-boiled automotive economists forecast 50 million cars on the road by 1959. The fact is the 58,591,000 cars were registered in 1959. This forecasting error of approximately 8.6 million cars represents about half the passenger cars in Western Europe.

We failed to anticipate many factors that affect housing. By the late nineteen-forties, we did include playgrounds in city apartments built for young families. But we did not foresee the number of cars they would buy. And we did not reckon with the demand for television sets, automatic washing machines, and air conditioners that made these building electrically obsolete while they were still new. Most serious of almost city apartments do not have enough bedrooms for the baby crop. So the young families move out to the suburbs.

But they aren't much better off in the suburbs either. There are enough bedrooms of babies in the typical two-bedroom house built in this '40's. And many lack garages and carports. Young owners invest million trying to expand their little homes. Many give up and move out. Thanks to the automobile and the rise in real income, they can move still further from town, to find more space in the far suburbs in new homes they soon outgrow once again.

Business planers in the suburbs also failed to anticipate our growth. Many post-war shopping centers allowed only two square feet of parking space for every square foot of selling space. But today often ratio of firm square feet to one square foot is required.

As a result..

The 600-mile city arrives unherablded.

One of the main characteristics of this dynamic growth is the rapid evolution of the now-familiar phenomenon known as Suburbia into as infinitely more complex social pattern now known as INTERURBIA.

The most graphic demonstration of this evolution is in New York City. There, as elsewhere, it is no longer quite realistic to speak of a city and is suburbs. The New York metropolitan area has long been a conglomeration of many cities and many suburbs. Interms of population and physics plant, the "city" goes beyond the already obsolete limits of the New York metropolitan area. Indeed, it is no longer a Greater New York of a Greater Boston, Philadelphia, Baltimore or Washington. It is virtually about 600-mile city from Maine to Virginia. Actually, there are only two stretches in this 600-mile city—one of 2 miles, the other of 17 miles which are not part of metropolitan areas. And while this 600-mile "city" comprises less than 2 per cent of its nation's land area, it represents 24 per cent of its retail sales.

Interurbia, by definition, has these characteristics: it contains two more adjacent metropolitan areas with either two cities of 100,000 more, or one city of 100,000 and 3 cities of 25,000 or more, plus adjacent counties with less than 25 per cent farm population and more than 100 people per square mile.

There are now 14 of these Interurbias in the U.S. based on the last Census—plus two Interurbias in the making in the Southwest. They dot the landscape of the Eastern Seaboard, Midwest, Southwest and Pacific Coast. Together they account of or almost half of the country's population of 178 million and for more than half of its retail sales, yet they stand on less than 4 per cent of the country's total land. Within these fourteen interurbias, an average of 620 people live in every square mile—over 12 times as many people per square mile as there are in the rest of the country.

There are also some areas that did not at the last censure quite fit the definition of an Interurbia, but that almost certainly will fit it soon.

One of these is long the Florida coast and across the middle of the peninsula. North of Miami the coastal strips is already filled in for many miles. A big Interurbian growth is now under way south of Tampa and is beginning to touch the Fort Myers area. By 1965, this Interurbia will probably account for two thirds of the population of Florida.

Another potential Interurbia is to be found in the Piedmont area. So far this long chain of cities has reflected only the first stage of urbanization. Cities have grown faster than surrounding country. And there are long groups of open country between many of the cities. But the area is growing letter than the states it lies in and shows signs of becoming an Interurbia in the near future.

The plantation is quite simple, although the results are incredibly complicated. What has happened is that homes and jobs, at one time closely tied to each other and firmly fixed in their places, have both been made movable—as tough at the end of increasingly long ropes.

The central fact which distinguishes Interurbia from suburbia is that that labour force does not move in a steady one-way stream, but more in a prices of cross currents. Westport, Connecticut, in Northeastern Interurbia serves as an example.

Most people commuting from West port move southwesterly to New York, but a significant percentage commute to Bridgeport, and New York. And Westport itself also receives part of its own labour force from Connecticut, nearby New York and the surrounding countryside.

The emergence of Interurbia from the now out-dated concept of city, and country has been stimulated more by the growth of satellite cities than it has from the big central city. The Interurbia in the Chicago and Milwaukee area or strip serves to illustrate this fact.

Between 1930 and 1959 the population in the suburban areas between Chicago and Milwaukee proper has increased 95 per cent while the cities themselves have increased 17 per cent. The same is true of the retail sales. In the areas between Chicago-Milwaukee, retail sales in 1959 were 460 per cent greater than in 1930, while in the two cities themselves, retail sales had increased 167 per cent.

What is true in the suburban areas in the Chicago-Milwaukee strip appears to be true of the entire country. In 1958, dollar sales per capita in the Interurbian suburbs were, on the average, 68 per cent higher than in the other suburbs of the country.

Interurbia in 1975

As we look to the future, we can with some confidence, predict the day is not too far distant when most of our people will be passed within Interurbia—as most of our sales now are. In 1975, it is estimated that Interurbia will represent 60 per cent of our population 70 per cent of retail sales.

Our 600-mile city in the Northeast may well grow toward the paramount. Its arm now creeping up the Hudson, will in all probability with Cleveland, Detroit, and Chicago, and stretch down Illionois to Louis. That would be an Interurbia about twice the length of the Atlantic strip—a city more than 1,200 miles long.

On the West Coast, the future holds the distinct possibility of an urban strip stretching northward from San Diego and connecting somewhere in the Caligornia Valley with the southward movement from San Francisco and the Bay area.

In the South, Dallas and Fort Worth extend in one direction down to Housston and Galveston, and in another, through Waco and Austin to San Antonio.

People will, as in the past, settle close to water ways, whether they be ocean, lake, river, or canal; but there will be other motivations, too—climate, the need for land and, as always, the desire for better living.

How Interurbia may affect Our Way of Living

Beneath the shell of uniform mass housing there most likely will be a series of different communities each catering to a different age and income group. The trend toward physical uniformity is rating a counter desire to be socially different. And this desire to be different is already apparent in some of the ostensibly homogeneous suburbs a such as the Levittowans in the East and in Park Forest, south of Chicago.

Families are on the move. More and more people are leaving the old home town—in a series of moves—from home won to college, from college to a great organization, and then from one provincial outpost to another, until finally comes the day when the man is summoned home to Rome.

The old home town may look pretty much the same. Yet if you check the leadership in the traditional town, you will find that the sons of the "early" families have more often than not left to join the transient life. Someone else, very much like them, is now sitting in the place they might have had in the Junior Chamber of commerce, the Community Chest, or the Greens Committee of the Country Club.

Then there is the more familiar kind of mobility—the great exodus from the city to the country. Familiar, yes, except that the exodus does not necessarily consist of just one jump—from city to suburbs.

To illustrate: since the war, there has been a tremendous growth in row-house developments in Northeast Philiadelphia. Socially, however, for many of these people there is still another transition to be made. For all their boasting about what a wonderful place the "5600" block is, the unspoken goal is to move out of the city. If the husband gets that raise, the "For Sale' sign goes up.

Mobility breeds more mobility. Once a person has learned to change environment it becomes easier to adapt to another. The good transient is professional about this.

Another aspect of this mobility is the tremendous upgrading urge it produces. One of the most characteristic complaints to be found in the new villages of Interurbia is about the quality of goods they have in the stores. The complaint usually takes the lines of 'who-do-they-thing-we-are-anyway?"

The most interesting thing about this upgrading urge is how very much it is conditioned by the immediate group in which a couple find themselves.

It is the group in Interurbia that determines when a luxury becomes a necessity. Take something like an automatic dryer. When only a few housewives in a block have one, other h6usewives can take it or leave it. As more and more housewives follow suit, it soon becomes an almost unsocial act not to own one. Finally only the most resolute can hold out. This use to improve one's own status has caused the developer of one of the new suburbs to suggest somewhat facetiously building a "life cycle suburb." You would live in one court as a child, a two bedroom apartment as a newlywed: then a ranch house; final, then you're old and gray, and your children are scattered to the four winds, you would move back to a court to serve out your term as a baby sitter.

Interurbian Psychology

Do the psychological needs of the people living in Interurbia difficult from those in the rest of the country? They do most decidedly. Here from a special study of several thousand people, are the principal derives of these Interurbian people and some idea a to how they may differ five the rest of the population.

The Interurbian man is significantly above the national average in his expressed desire for achievement—his desire to rival and surpass others—to do hi best—to achieve prestige and acclaim. He has an equally pronounced need to dominate other people. He wants to be a leader influence others. The Interurbian man is more willing to talk about and less strict in his attitudes.

Our Interurbian man likes also to be the center of attention—to have others notice him-to make an impression on others. In short, vanity and self-dramatization are stronger needs in him than they are in the living elsewhere in our land. Change he doesn't mind. In fact, tour Interest bian man likes to do new and different things...to change his daily routine. He likes variety and novelty. Possibly this is a key as to why accepts the need for mobility with such calm.

It is a fact of great significance in the development of future advertising appeals that the characteristics which are most highly developed in the men and women of Interurbia are those on which so many great advertising success stories have been built and will be built. The people of Interurbia might be said to represent a pre-conditioned audience for the skillful advertising of many products and services to a greater degree than the people outside Interurbia.

How Interurbia Stimulates and Stabilizes our Economy

Interurbia will push us toward a national economy that certainly will be bigger, and probably more stable. The stability will be due to the changing pattern of ownership and consumption interurbia imposes. Except for a little furniture and a closet full of clothes, most Interurbia city dwellers have no passions. New York city, for example, accounts for only three per cent of the nation's automobiles, but represents 15 per cent of the country's restaurant sales.

By contrast, the Interurbiate who has left the big city is forced to become a man of property. His ownership of a house creates a hunger for hard goods that inevitably drives him into hard work more relentlessly than the metropolitan dweller.

For example, one large builder found that the purchase of every new home automatically created 17 other purchases, such as furniture, appliances, curtains, garden tools, a new car-even a second car.

The stabilizing influence of Interurbia also arises from the huge spending programme on the part of businesses, utilities and public authorities that interurbia demands. And Interurbia's need for new highways alone is accelerating the need for housing in a brutally direct fashion. The present highway construction programme calls for the destruction or removal of about 90,000 houses a year—just to build roads!

Still another stabilizing influence lies in the increased opportunity for workers to maintain employment by being more mobile.

While the automobile has become the symbol of many Inerurbian problems, it fills a basic need. The phenomenon of Interurbia is based on the mobility supplied by the private car to drive miles to shopping center school, church and job. If anything, the need for this mobility will grow as business and homes spread further out.

But the growing use of the automobile is outstripping

the ability of the central city to cope with it. In fact, the congestion has become so overpowering that some planners are persuaded that the means taken to open the choked downtown arteries are mere expedients. Some are bold enough to predict a not-too-distant day when the private car is barred altogether from the metropolitan city, as an improved intra-city barred altogether from the metropolitan city, as an improved intra-city transit system takes on the job of moving people about faster than they are now moving.

New Marketing Problems

The marketing problems created by Interurbia will be no less complex. With 31,000,000 changes of residence every year, the retailer worrying about new locations will have to keep a close watch on consumer movements.

The friendly neighbourhood dealer may lose some of his old sales punch as he sees new faces among his customers more often than before.

The manufacturer may find that the Central Cities in Interurbia are no longer the focus of marketing, but somewhere in between. Test marketing may be expanded to Interurbian strips, instead of individual markets. The same may be true do product research.

Sales organizations may grow smaller, as they concentrate more retail service. The two-thousand-man sales force may become a thing of the past.

Executives in charge of areas with traditional designations such as New England, Middle Atlantic, may be re-assigned to supervise a particular Interurbian strip.

New stores, service stations, and discount houses will expose customers to brands they've never seen before. As New York and Boston toward each other in the nation's largest Interurbia, they carry with these certain brands that New London, Connecticut, had never herd of. That same may apply to prices. Discount houses will introduce some cut price hitherto unknown to various communities along the way.

The Interurbian shopper for a refrigerator or other hard goods may soon be shopping in a retail store which carries no stock except the needed for demonstration or display. The retailer will simply phone in order to a warehouse, and the model ordered will be on the truck delivered to the customer's house within a matter of hours.

This new convenience for the retail shopper within Interurbia will made possible through a mammoth warehouse system handling may brands and a variety of product. It is conceivable, for example, that the hard-goods' needs of Northeast Interurbia alone could be efficiently supplied by four or five such warehouses.

The Interurbian influence can already be detected in the marketing procedures of many important good chains. The central city is no longer the sole location for their warehousing and buying. Rather their never centers have either moved out from eh metropolitan area, or they are being duplicated out in the growing Interurbian territory.

Even today, in major chains like Kroger and Colonial stores, we find some warehouse buying headquarters outside the central city with well developed "spokes" that are completely independent of any historic city or political boundaries.

As we change from the old concept of a metropolitan marketing area to a new Intrurbian marketing area, perhaps we should re-examine the traditional methods by which we separate and study our markets.

Perhaps it may not be too early for market research firms to break down their findings on the basis of interurbia versus non-Interurbia.

Advertising Media in Interurbia

Concentration of population has virtually always meant lower advertising costs. The bigger the mass of circulation an advertiser buyers, the lower the relative cost to him.

Today the space an advertiser buys in a country weekly can cost him ten times as much per unit of circulation as the space in a large daily. As interurbia develops, this discrepancy may be narrowed—with increased efficiency in advertising expenditure.

In the new Interurbia, the metropolitan daily may, of necessity, become less and less identified with the central city of Interurbia, and more with Interurbia as a whole. One ay of accomplishing this is to publish more zoned editions, as some large dailies are already doing.

The smaller dailies and weeklies may stand to benefit from the Interurbian development in two ways: first, they are in the happy position of serving their readers come to them; secondly, the pattern of marketing is changing so fast that major chain stores are becoming less and less identified with the central city, as they develop new spokes in their marketing wheel.

Interurbia also presents a challenge to Sunday supplements, whose substantial post-war growth has been based on their ability to provide coverage of the large metropolitan centers. More and more, the supplements may find it beneficial to buttress their circulation in the medium-size cities between their present major metropolitan markets. This would enable them to provide the same intensive coverage of the Interurbian areas that they now provide in central cities.

Today some 70 national magazines representing 71% of all audited magazine circulation accept advertising for circulation covering individual regions or markets. This trend of magazines toward regional adverting may gain further momentum as more advertisers begin to look at circulations for whole Interurbias, and not just their metropolitan segments. In so doing, they will find in many cases that the traditionally broad-base magazines can cover as many or more families within Interurbia as some of the individual local media that they have used traditionally.

TV set ownership throughout Interurbia will increase to something close to the 90 per cent that now exists in metropolitan areas. But TV network structures still lag behind the Interurbian development due to their historical tie to individual markets. Thus an advertiser seeking coverage of Northeastern Interurbia would have to supplement his ten network stations with several spot stations. Further network requirements for "must-buy" TV stations may be related more directly to Interurbias.

Comparative Advertising hits Retail Trade

Food bazaar cries foul at Subhiksha's comparative ads, while Big Bazaar goes comparative on its competitors

When advertising gets aggressive and highly competitive, one of two things can happen. Competitors will react strongly, or they won't react at all. That's what is happening in retail, with Food Bazaar reacting strongly to a comparative attack on the one hand, and sister concern Big Bazaar doing a comparative attack on competition on the other hand. Subhiksha, the low price chain, is on an aggressive expansion spree. It recently came out with a print ad campaign, comparing its own prices with competition's. The ads wouldn't have raised so much of a rucks normally. "Subhiksha" says its MD, R. Subramanian, "regularly publishes comparative prices."

However, this time, Food Bazaar, owned by the Future Group, has taken Subhiksha to the advertising Standards Council of India (ASCI), protesting about its campaign. Food Bazaar's CEO, Sadashiv Naik, says, "There's no harm in comparing prices if the comparison is consistent. But the Subhiksha campaign compares its prices for some food items in certain cities with the prices of our food items in another city this is an inconsistent comparison." Why ASCI, question Subramanian? "If they feel that our advertising is not fair, they could have also gone to The Monopolies and Restrictive trade Practices Commission." He adds that Food Bazaar's tagline, "*Isse sasta aur accha kahin nahin*" is misleading. "For get us, their prices are higher than D-Mart too and we were just stating this fact."

Naik shrugs off he outburst: "That's Subhiksha's viewpoint. All that we wanted to do was bring the inconsistencies to ASCI's notice." Even as Food Bazaar fights a comparative advertising battle with Subhiksha, Big Bazaar has launched an aggressive hoardings campaign, taking comparative pot-shots, at Shoppers' Stop, Lifestyle and Westside.

Prominently displayed messages such as "Shoppers! Stop. "Change your Lifestyle" and "Keep West Aside" stare motorists in the face in Mumbai.

Big Bzaar's CEO, Rajan Malhotra, defends the campaign: "There's nothing offensive about the ads as the first line below the headline says that we're only advertising the fact that one can get inexpensive products at Big Bazaar and don't mean to offend any competitors." He adds that Big Bazaar used to come out with four page booklets at intervals. This time, we thought hat we should do something different." And is competition reacting? "We honestly have no comment to give on the new Big Bazaar campaign," Sheetal Choksi, Shoppers' Stop's customer care associate and vice-president marketing & communication, says.

A case of ignore-it-and-it-will-go-away, or is it that not reacted cuts down the aggressor's impact than would have been the case otherwise.

2

Process of Marketing Management

The Marketing plan requires coordination of the finance, production, consumer behaviour, distribution, pricing approach and staffing factors in an organization, to ensure support with adequate money, material, machines and manpower (4Ms). Thus, the marketing management process may be defined as the function of business opportunities, research, designing marketing strategies, planning marketing programmes, implementation and control factors. The stages of the marketing management process is exhibited as under:

1. Assessment of business opportunity
2. Organising research, market surveys
3. Selecting target markets
4. Strategy formulation
5. Planning marketing programmes
6. Implementation
7. Controlling marketing efforts.

The marketing managers have to carry out their responsibilities integrating all these factors in the management process. A manager needs to build and operate a marketing information system into confidence to identify and evaluate the appropriate business opportunities. Thus, marketing research is an important and indispensable component of the modern marketing concept. The variables that need to be analysed for identifying business opportunities are broadly listed below:

1. Product characteristics
2. Status of substitute and complimentary products
3. Segmented markets
4. Consumers profiled
5. Potential market locations
6. Emerging distribution points
7. Distribution network
8. Competition, threats, and demand fluctuations
9. Pricing policy of similar products and anticipated changes for the new entries in the market
10. User reactions on product announcements in the market
11. User response to similar products
12. Anticipated turnover of the product in terms of quantity and value
13. Scope of market segmentation
14. Market promotion possibilities
15. Scope of the product or price leadership.

The identification of appropriate opportunities require a logical interpretation of the results of marketing research. The marketing managers have to user their discretion in identifying such opportunities keeping in view the market environment. The business opportunity may also be located on the product-positioning map plotted on the axis of competitive products status. The product-positioning map is exhibited with the help of the quality price matrix. The illustration reveals that the decision on the product positioning, which is also an implication on effective marketing planning, can be taken on the basis of plotting the price and quality matrix in reference to different types of products or companies operating in the market with their products and sixes of business. The decision has to be taken for the positioning of competitor of the company in view of the prevailing position so f four competitors A,B, and D. Competitor A sells his high quality products at high prices performing a smaller size of business as compared to other competitors. Competitor B appears to be performing below average business, as he is engaged in selling low quality products at a low price, while the competitor 'C' holds a 'rip off status being engaged in selling low quality of products at a higher price. In all, competitor 'D' stands an average status of balance, making a decision between the price and quality factors. Now, the analysis reveals that competitor 'E' who is a new entry to the market may position hi products provided, he compromises to sell the high quality products at lower prices. However, the span of the compromise is subject to the product recognition and level of the customers recognizing the product and endorsing the degree of satisfaction. Such an approach of product positioning may be termed as 'dumping' anzt in a short term. The competitor may shift the position later to HQ-HP status and run the business with segmented consumers.

As stated in the pretext, the product positioning is a function related to product-consumer symbiosis in terms of quality, price, availability and more significantly the user perceptions on its satisfaction. The case of Green Hair Tonic is discussed in the competitive market.

Marketing Segmentation

This is one of the prerequisites for planning the marketing activities for any product. Segmenting, targeting and positioning (STP) are the three basic components of strategic marketing in modern times. Segmentation of market is a process of identifying the agglomeration of buyers their wants, purchasing power, geographical locations, their buying attitudes and behaviour, to facilitate the targeting and positioning of the products It is essential to identify the segmentation variables and developing profiles of the resulting segmentation for marketing decision for marketing planning. Broadly, it can be stated that the market segments are the large groups within the market, while a niche is a more arrowly defined group seeking for additional marketing benefits. There are many bases for segmenting the consumer markets. The territorial segmentation I done in terms of region like countries, continents or sub-continent and the habit identification is made as villages, towns, cities and metro spread geographically according to the size of the population. In the demographic category of segmentation, the density of population, composition of population, family size, occupational distribution, level of education and population categories in terms of religion and other sects are considered. The psychographic variables of market segmentation consists of nationality of the consumers, their race like black, white, Aryans, Dravidians, Buddhists etc. The social class of the consumers viz., forward, backward or aboriginal class is also used as a variable of market segmentation. Besides the above variables, the lifestyle of the consumers and their personality also provide rich information for segmenting the consumer markets. In the behavioural variable category, apart from other variables, the personal preferences make a substantial impact in identifying the consumer segments for the products. Te personal preference can be categorized in the following three patterns:

- Homogeneous preferences for the products or brands
- Diffused preferences showing greater variations for the brands across the regions
- Clustered preferences indicating localised preferences of the consumers for the brands available.

The information on the above listed variable for the market segmentation can be collected by conducting exploratory interviews and focus group analysis in order to gain the consumer insights on motivation, attributes and behavour. The data may be collected through the structured questionnaire comprising broadly the issues related to consumer behaviour, brand awareness and brand rating, product usage patterns, product mix behaviour, demographic and psychographic variables. The factor analysis may be applied to the data collected to find out highly correlated variable and through the cluster analysis, specified number of different segments can be identified. Each identified cluster can then be profiled in terms of distinguished variables used in the analysis. The market segmentation procedure must be applied periodically as the consumer segments keep changing due to external influences and personal preferences.

The procedure for segmenting he industrial marketing sis different than the consumer markets. However, the selected industrial market can be further segmented for the consumer goods. The major variable that need to be considered for the segmentation of the industrial markets.

The type of the industry, its size and locatio. constitutes the physical variables required for segmenting the industrial markets. The type of existing technology in use, future prospects, production capabilities, the target group of customers for the products of the industry and the policy of transportation, warehousing and inventory may be the operational variables used in determining the industrial marketing segments. Besides these, it is essential that the market planner knows to segment the industrial goods and services, as well as be aware of other factors like—the purchase policy of the industry, chances of any lobbying of suppliers, the extent of the relationship retained between the buyer and seller over a period of time and the criteria followed for the purchase of goods and services, large volume of order of the listed products of request to cater to specific tailor-made order, legal impositions of certain goods and services, newly emerged users or as a requirement of a substitute of a complementary product for the business or industry's use. Above all, the risk factoring penetrating such a market segment, brand loyalty among the user etc. are also important variable to make sense in the decision-making for segmenting the market for the industrial customers. In a given operational area for the company, the market for the consumer goods and services can be segmented in five different forms as detailed under:

- One product in one market: micro-consumer segmentation
- Different products in different markets: diffused segmentation
- All products in one market: specialized market segmentation
- Al products in all markets: absolution market segmentation or total coverage.

Marketing segmentation should be followed by the targeting and product positioning activities for effective planning and implementation of the marketing plans.

Marketing Planning

It may be denied as the scheduling of different activities related to product identification, pricing, placement and promotion in a synchronized manner for achieving the business goals of an organisation. It is further explained as a document or a guiding tool to execute the marketing programmes in the segmented markets. The plan needs to be drafted initially and finalised subject to its favourable results of pilot testing.

A marketing plan consists of four sub-plans pertaining to basic determinants, technical requirements, networking and contingencies. The planning process begins with an exhaustive baseling survey o the product to assess the demand opportunities for the product positioning, consumer behaviour. Market environment and competitive products. The survey analysis would help the managers to choose the right product for the right segment of consumer as well as decide its scope in the market among the competitive products. The opinion of the consumers would reveal the level of the product acceptance and the needed reforms for introducing it in the market stages involved in an effective marketing planning, that needs to be considered by the marketing managers for preparing the sales platform for a new product under competition. The results of the baseline survey would help in identifying the products and segmenting the market according to demand, competition and related variables. The product can be positioned in the segmented market and the targets be set accordingly. It is essential that the marketing plan should exercise financial flexibilities to meet the contingencies and cost involved in administering the strategic plans. Hence, the marketing budgeting plays a important role in administering the marketing plan. It consists of budgetary provisions on variable and fixed cost components viz., marketing personnel, agents, infrastructures, transport, product promotion and contingencies.

The marketing plan may be drafted on completing the chain of preplanning exercises and tested initially in the segmented market. A marketing manager is required to be appraised of the pilot product launching results for confirming the draft plan. The plan can later be implemented 'per se' or subject to modifications in view of the review of pilot testing. In the course of the mass launching of the product, it is required to water the market trend by an internal assessment, dong the SWOT exercise before implementing the draft marketing plan. However, a contingency plan would always be helpful to sustain the product marketing in case of uncertainties. An overall business review of the marketing plan may add some new dimension in relaunching the products following the cycled exercise again. This would be helpful in identifying the new market segments and relaunching the products which have reached the stage of 'aging' in the product cycle.

As stated in the pretext, a market plan consists of sub-plans and each sub-plan has many variables.

An integrated model of these sub-plans formulate an effective marketing plan. However, the business targets depend on the efficient implementation of the marketing plan. A marketing manager is required to enlist the marketing strategy for translating the marketing plan into success in the market. The strategy statement may be presented in a task-order manner.

Table 2.1: Variables of Marketing Sub-plan

Plan 1 Baseline research	*Plan 2 Technical plan*	*Plan 3 Organizational* plan	*Plan 4 Contingency* plan
* Survey of demand	* Advertising	* Distribution	* Market expansion
* Consumer behaviour	* Branding * Packaging	* Regulation * Managerial Infrastructure	* New products * Additonal alternative resources
* Market segmentation	* Sales incentives		
* Competitive pricing	* Quality control	* MIS	* Risk management
* Customer service	* Product line * Consumer awareness	* Public relations	* Diversification

1. Targeting market and product
2. Product positioning
3. Product line
4. Pricing
5. Distribution networking
6. Sales force
7. Customer service
8. Product promotion
9. Market expansion
10. Research and development
11. Market appraisal, monitoring and evaluation.

In developing a strategy, the manager is required to discuss it with others whole cooperation is sought for making the implementation of the plan a success. An action programme has to be drawn on thrust areas and its 'modus operandi be designed. The manager, in doing so, also needs to ensure that the action programme retains the quality of cot-effectiveness.

Allocation of Marketing Resource

Logistics of investment in marketing is an important consideration in planning the product marketing strategies. In the process, the resources identified for the investment need to be emphasized as 'how to generate' and 'when to invest' and 'how to optimize returns on investment'. In all, 'profit' is the principal resource in the business being used for expansion, diversification and reformative measures in product marketing. However, the manager also has t ensure that the capital borrowed from external sources need to be invested as logically as profit to optimize the net returns on the investment. The extent of profit depends on the marketing expenditure on different variables like list price, price spread (allowances per unit such as freight changes, commission, transport, discount, incidental costs etc.), variable costs related with production and distribution, quantity of sales, fixed cost such as rent, taxes etc. and discretionary marketing costs. A difference between the gross contribution margin and cost including fixed costs and discretionary marketing costs accounts for total profits of the company or an organisation. Mathematically, it can be expressed in the following force.

$$P_g = [(P_1 \text{-} P_{s)} — V_c] \; Q_n \text{-} (F_c + x) \text{ ---- (i)}$$

P_g = Gross profit

P_1 = List price of product

P_s = Price spread (freight charges, commission etc.)

Q_n = Sales quantity (No. of units)

X = Incidental costs

V_c = Variable cost, including production & marketing

F_r = Fixed costs

In the above equation, the segment $[(P_1 - P_s) - V_c]q_n$ represents per unit profit contributed, which results in gross profit, if multiplied with the quantity of products sold in the market. The profit assessment is one of the exercises, in the resource allocation task as it contributes the major share of investment capital. Besides, it is necessary for a manager to prioritise the areas of investment and allocate the budgetary weightages to make the resource planning effective.

A manager is required to classify the capital available for investment under different sources and provide weightage to allocate the resources for investment with prioritized areas. In order to optimize the profit and generate adequate resources, it is essential to view the impact of the marketing-mix components on sales. The 'sales response function' describes the relationship of sales volume with a particular component of the marketing mix. It is a symbiosis and each element of the mix forecasts the volume of sales in reference to time holding other constant. The relationship of sales volume, market expenditure and profit influences the gross profit status of an organisation. The net-profit is the variable emerging from the difference between the total marketing expenditure and the gross profit values.

Profit Planning

Having attended all logical considerations in the marketing planning, profit in and business organization should not be left to change. It needs to be properly planned with future perspectives. The steps a manager needs to take to achieve an effective profit goal are:

States of Profit Planning (Primary Level)

1. To establish a profit goal
2. Setting up planned volume of sales
3. Assess expenditure on targeted volume of sales
4. Draw profit estimation based on the plans of sales targets and expenditure to achieve these targets.

In the initial stages of a business, a manager can end his profit planning process at this stage. However, he may further improve the plan, in regard to the growth of sales volume and enhanced marketing objectives of the organisation. In the profit planning process, often, the problem of accuracy in data of various sales expenditure is observed which misrepresents the results for profits f unknown quantity or sometimes losses. However, the following steps would be further helpful in determining, profit and understanding the impact of expenditure item on profit generation.

Stages of Profit Planning

1. Alternative plans for improving profitability level
2. Assessment of fluctuations in marketing expenditure in reference to targeted volume of sales and vice versa
3. Expedite profit potentials in different markets
4. Make larger budgetary provisions for enhanced marketing expenditure to tap participated profit go as and modify the profit plan accordingly.

A precaution has to be taken by the manager while passing through these advanced planning stages in order to avoid the market and product bias of customers. Thus, be realistic in exercising the profit planning step. However, profit is always risk averse, hence, uncertainty in achievements may occur. Broadly, profit planning needs to be down with a realistic approach to the optimum level of expectation. Peter Drucker states that "profits are the risk premium covering the costs of staying in business, the future source of capital, inspiration for innovation and growth in economy and necessary in business." In a business organisation, profit-oriented marketing is considered as an operational objective which is one among the hierarchical objectives of an organization.

In achieving these objectives, an organisation often

runs into many 'trade-off situations, where a logical decision is required to be taken by the manager. These 'trade-offs' are:

1. Short-run profits Vs. long-term growth
2. High volume of sales Vs. high profit margins
3. Product penetration Vs. product diversification
4. Market intensification Vs. market expansion
5. Quantitative parameters Vs. customer satisfaction goals
6. Profiteering philosophy Vs. social marketing practices
7. Lightning impact Vs. sustainability
8. Subsistence profit Vs. risk avers operations
9. High growth Vs. status quo' in the market.

Hence a business has to be developed on compatible strategies to web off the state of confusion. However, commonly a business company aims at long-term benefits, it has to forego short-run profit bargains for the sake of customer relationships. Such a transitory period in business builds up high economic pressure on the organisation.

Process of Marketing Strategy

Secondly, identifying the integrative growth opportunities with a view to build or acquire the related business for strengthening the principal mission. The company may develop plans at this stage for backward and forward integration and horizontal integration. Finally, looking for the diversification of growth opportunities which provide an attractive scope off business. Such areas of business may not necessarily match with the current business. The diversification growth opportunities can be planned by the company in view of the concentric, horizontal and conglomerative changes in the business. The Market-Opportunity Probability Matrix. The company, following the concentric strategy seeks new products that have technological and/or marketing syneries with the existing product-lines, even though the products may appeal to the new class of customers. In developing the conglomerative strategies, the company attempts to seek new business which have no relevance to the existing technology, products or markets.

The business opportunities can be listed and categorized as per the attractiveness, economic gains and the success probabilities. The company may develop extensive market plans if the attractiveness of the opportunity and economic gains are high as well as thee exists a high probability of success. On the contrary to this alliance, the company may not hurry up in investing time and money to realize such opportunities. The company needs a strong drive (pool of effectivemanagers0 to implement the marketing plan. The marketing manager should be proactive to the market demands, customer needs, complaints and redressal. Besides, the monitoring and evaluation system need to be developed and ensured by the company towards quality control, human resources deployment, task allocation and developing ad hoc strategies. However, the goal of the company should be to achieve the optimal customer satisfaction. The customer and channel feedback need to be taken periodically and analysed. The points of change in he management strategy should be inducted under intimation to the target customers or channel managers. Such endorsement on the feedback in changing the strategies could develop confidence in the company and encourage participatory dynamics. The company while implementing the marketing plans should keep in mind the related objectives other than the customer satisfaction, are the long-term customer retention and augmenting the market share of the company's goods and services. The company should account for the 4Cs comparising customer needs, cost to customers, convenience and communication to the customers while developing the marketing plans.

Marketing plan is an important tool for developing profit oriented approaches and also a referral document for the business organisation all through its existence in the market. This document has to be prepared and used scientifically. It contains many sections as under:

1. Executive summary
2. Business profile
3. Existing marketing situation
4. Marketing objectives
5. Opportunities and strategies analysis : (i) Target market (ii) Positioning (iii) Product-line (iv) Price (v)distribution (vi) Sales force (vii) Service (viii) Advertising (ix) Sales promotion (x) Research & development (xi) Marketing research (xii) Feedback and control (xiii) Relaunch.
6. Action programme
7. Problems foreseen
8. Alternative marketing plans
9. Profit Statement
10. Monitoring and control.

The executive summaryshoudl contain the marketing objectives, trust areas action programme and future perspectives. Itisused as a brief sketch of the organisaton. Tehmain body of document should begin with the buiness profile indicatignthe results of baseline survey, product,demnd potential, proposed segmented markets, coparative advantages of theproductandfuture perspective. The marketingsituton needs to be analysed with the followigntheme of thpln document focusingonthe competition scenario, product network, supplymecanisms, price structure, consumer awareness, trde brick-bats, promotional patternadopted by the competitors. The marketing opportunities and strategies constitute the most dynamic part of the document and need to be dealt in detail in the following order.

The strategies must explain the market-mix pattern, resource allocation, profit planning, product diversification plan etc. However, an observation on the anticipated problems of marketing would be beneficial toad in the plan document after the strategies are discussed. The document must also endorse the alternative strategies in view of the problems foreseen. The profit plans need to be described in the plan document, subject to regulations and should never be considered as a laissez faire. Hence it is necessary to build upon effective monitoring and control mechanism in the business.

Marketing as a social and managerial process by which individuals and groups obtain what they need and want through creating and exchanging products and value with others. The term market originates from the Latin word Marcatus which means a place where business is conducted. It is not simply a place of exchange but an arrangement that provides an opportunity for exchanging goods and services for money. We have to examine the following terms—needs, wants and demands, products, value and satisfaction, exchange, transactions and relationships and markets.

The basic concept underlying marketing is that of human needs. Man has different types of needs such as physical needs for food and clothing, social needs for love and affection and individual needs for knowledge and self-expression. When a need is not satisfied, people will develop object that will satisfy their needs. People have unlimited wants but limited resources. They will choose the products that will provide the most satisfaction for their money. When backed up by purchasing power, wants become demands. People satisfy their needs and wants with products. A product is anything which can satisfy a want or need. Products include physical products as well as services. Consumers generally face a number of products that might satisfy a given need. Consumers make buying decisions. On the basis of their perceptions of a product's value, the consumer will choose the product that will give him the most benefit for his money.

Marketing occurs when people decide to satisfy needs

and wants through exchange. Exchange is the act of getting a desired object from someone by offering something in return. Exchange is the core concept of marketing whereas a transaction is marketing's unit of measurement. Transaction consists of a trade value between two parties. Transactions may be monetary transaction or barter transaction. Transaction marketing is part of the larger idea of relationship marketing. Progressive marketers try to build long-term relationships with valued customers, distributors, dealers and suppliers. They build strong economic and socialities by promising maximum benefits. The concept of transactions leads to the concept of a market. A market is the set of actual and potential buyers of a product. A market can grow up around a product, a service or anything else of value. Hence there are labor market, money market or donor market. The concept of markets finally completes the circle of the concept of marketing. Marketing means working with markets to bring about exchanges for the purpose of satisfying human needs and wants.

Concepts of Market

Place Concept: A market is a convenient meeting place for buyers and sellers to come together to carry on buying and selling activities.

Area Concept: A Market develops in an area, the moment there are three preconditions for exchange: (a) Two or more individuals with unsatisfied wants (b) They have products or services to exchange and (c) They have some means of communications such as telephone, telex, e-mail correspondence, etc.

Demand Concept: The term market is also used to represent total customer demand. In this sense, market means people with needs to satisfy the money to spend and they will to spend money to satisfy their needs.

Marketing Management Functions

The achievement of predetermined marketing goals

requires integrates and coordination of all market-related elements of the firm. Marketing management's task is to combine these elements into an effective creating system and to manage the system in its interaction with a dynamic environment. Marketing management functions that must be informed to plan and manage a corporate marketing system are assigning marketing opportunity, planning and programming marketing actively, actuating marketing organization and leadership, and evaluating and adjusting marketing effort.

Assessing of marketing opportunity involves the identification of company goals and the analysis of established and new profit opportunities be the firm. The significance of this function is that market opportunities continually changing, and marketing management must develop creates strategies to cultivate these market opportunities. A planned program innovation is essential for marketing effectiveness. The firm must be expand to the market and adopt a broad and dynamic view of marketing opportunity. Performance of the assessment function on a continuing basis the firm that it will be dynamic in its marketing and production sections, that identification of the set of challenges and problems facing the company is possible, and that changing marketing opportunities will set effectively by the firm.

Meaning is an integral component of the marketing management scope and is a vital element of he systems orientation. This function, when based on the assessment of market opportunity, is a key successful marketing management and performance. Market planning used to develop and define objectives and then derive programmes that enable the firm to achieve these objectives. The systems approach quires a concise statement of these goals and encourages a system analysis of the impact of the programs devised. Planning provides the best for an integrated and coordinated marketing strategy. Coordination of the firm's marketing programmes is a must if the planned objectives of the business are to be achieved. To make planning central to the marketing concept, both sort-and long-range planning are involved.

The innovistic and dynamic nature of marketing activity places demands on the marketing organization. The systems approach influence the firm's thinking about the marketing organization. Viewing the organization as a goal-directed system can stimulate fundamental thinking about the firm's marketing operations and problems. The interaction process between the organization and the environment is a central concern of the marketing discipline. Application of the newer organizational theories have an impact on marketing operations. New product developments and the growing importance of international marketing are some of the marketing changes that have raised organizational problems for the firm Implementation of the marketing management concept will be direct reflected in the organizational changes that occur.

Diverse changes are influencing the patterns and styles of leader required for effective performance of marketing functions. Developments of newer patterns of leadership are testing traditional views of management methods and practices. For example, one organizational problem is raised by the tendency toward centralization of responsibility for integration the total marketing task. Balanced against this centralization tendency the need for greater participation in management and decision making people at subordinate levels. A solution requires analysis of management philosophy, communication patterns, the scope of responsibility authority, leadership abilities and staffing policies and practices, and development of appropriate policies in the setting of the individual section and firm.

In order to take advantage of profitable marketing opportunities marketing manager must continually evaluate and adjust the market effort. The firm must adjust to its ever-changing environment. An effective judgment, the marketing manager must have knowledge the entire marketing system so that the components of the system evaluated, controlled, and adjusted to bring the system in to line of the marketing opportunity. Essentially the major challenge confirmed marketing management is that of creative adaptation to change. This challenge, the firm should have a complete appraisal of its marketing operations through a marketing audit. The continuing problems of marketing management is to match marketing effort with marketing opportunity.

Nature and Dimension of Marketing

Marketing is the most important business activity because it links the two basic economic functions of production and consumption. Trade in the sense of exchange of goods and services is as old as civilization itself. But trade as such is different from marketing. Trade takes place after production but marketing precedes and pervades production and even follow up trade or exchange. Some definitions of marketing are given below with a view to highlighting its nature. The American Marketing Association defines marketing as the performance of business activities that direct the flow of goods and services from producer to consumer or users.

Marketing as the process which links producers and consumers by enabling transactions of exchange to take place to the mutual and continuing benefit of both parties—Robert Maxwell.

Edward Cundiff and Richard Still defines, marketing activities are those most directly concerned with the demand-stimulating and demand fulfilling efforts of the enterprise. These activities interlock and interact with one another as components of the total system—by which a company develops and makes its products available, distributes them through marketing channels—promotes them and prices them. In others words, marketing is concerned with product-market interrelationships and transfers of ownership.

Interrelationships

Product-market: Marketing is the business process by which products are matched with markets. Marketing and production activities are interlocked—we can market products that can be produced and we should only produce those that can be marketed.

Ownership Transfer: Ownership transfers occur repeatedly as products flow from producers to final buyers. A manufacturer may sell its output to wholesalers who, in turn resell to retailers who, again in turn, resell to consumers. In this case, every unit of the manufacturer's product that is finally purchased by a consumer has had its ownership transferred three times (from manufacturer to wholesaler, from whole seller to retailer and from retailer to consumer). There can be no marketing unless ownership transfers are effected.

Marketing as a Concept: By viewing a business through the eyes of the customers. The continued property of a firm can be ensured by providing the customers will 'value satisfaction' at a profit, satisfying their needs rather than simply selling what the firm has to offer. In other words, marketing is an organizational attitude which puts the customer at the centre of the decision-making process. The marketing concept recognizes the truth of Adam Smith's Dictum that Consumption is the sole purpose of all production. What this simple statement means in practices is that effective organizations must focus their attention externally upon customer needs and customer satisfaction and not simply internally upon products and production processions. This is because customers do not buy products or services. What they actually buy is utility—what the products and services purchased will do for them. So for marketers that key point of focus is not upon what is produced or delivered but rather upon the benefits and satisfactions that products and services can provide. The marketing concept calls upon organizations to recognize that it is the customer who determines what a business is. What the business thinks it produces is not of first importance. What the customer thinks he is buying or what he considers value, is decisive.

Marketing should be viewed as not merely a departmental function, but a guiding philosophy for the whole organization. The marketing concept calls for the whole organization to accept the truth of Drucker's assertion that 'there is only one valid definition of business purpose—to create a customer.'

The customer receives special attention because markets have two dynamics—competition and environmental change—which cannot be ignored. Most markets today are highly competitive. It means that the customer always has an alternative source of available supply. Unless the marketers understand the customers' needs and meet them effectively, then the customers will simply walk away. The customers should not be taken for granted. The other reason to be market-oriented is the fact of constant environmental change. This means that markets, customers and competition are constantly changing shape. Unless we are market-oriented, we have no way of keeping pace with change and our customers can slip from our group.

Marketing Functions

It is not enough to accept the marketing concept. It is also necessary to work out the definite ways in which customer satisfaction can be delivered. This is where the processor functions of marketing is critical. The marketing process is responsible for identifying, anticipating and satisfying customer, needs profitability. In practice, marketing process can be reduced to two crucial questions—who is our customer and how should we compete. The process of marketing begins with an attempt to understand the structure of the market place. It is not possible to attempt to appeal equally to all customers in all markets. Hence at the heart of the marketing process is the concept of market segmentation. The idea of a market as an economic obstruction of little practical use to the marketing. For this reason marketers seek to disaggregate overall markets into distinct and separate segments which can provide the basis for targeted marketing activity. The fist stage of the marketing process is the clear isolation of a clear target market. After the market has been satisfactorily segmented, the question is which segment should be selected as the organization's target market. The decision on where to compete is a key determinant of marketing success. We have to know who is our customer and what benefits does the customer seek.

The second question of our market offering concerns competition. Most industrial markets these days are highly competitive and what is needed for successful marketing is the development of a clear competitive advantage. Competitive advantage refers to a set of benefits which are superior to those of our major competitors.

In order to be competitive we need to know what our customers seek and what our competitors deliver. We can then build a sustainable competitive advantage. The sources of that competitive advantage are often described as the marketing mix. The marketing mix is a phrase used to describe the major operational variables which a marketing organization has under its control. These have traditionally been characterized as the product, price, promotion and place and people.

Marketing Techniques make the process possible. They include market research, pricing strategies, product development, distribution management and communication with the market and others.

Exchange is at the heart of marketing, without exchange marketing is redundant. The lowest form of economic organization is the subsistence economy. But this stage is devoid of a concept of marketing. Exchange first comes about where a producer creates a surplus in excess of the immediate needs of himself and his family, a surplus which he is willing to trade for some other goods. Any society which encourages specialization necessarily encourages exchange; Planned mixed and capitalist economies all share similar marketing problems. Each has physical distribution problems, each has mechanisms for determining what and how much should be produced; each has to make consumers aware of what is available an each has to set prices. Marketing techniques are applied irrespective of political structure. Marketing can be looked upon as an art, as a science and as a discipline. To define marketing a an art puts the emphasis on doing. To define marketing as a discipline stresses the academic side. To define marketing as a science is to see it as a body of knowledge with concepts, theories, principles and laws.

Evaluation and Adjustment of Marketing

Marketing must be treated as a total interacting system of business management, and the components of this system must be carefully evaluated and controlled. While a complete marketing audit may not be a feasible goal, much misplaced and misdirected marketing effort can be uncovered and corrected by a comprehensive analysis of sales volume and marketing costs.

The concept of an audit is not new to business management. Traditional it has carried the connotation of a review and evaluation of some sales activity. It has long been used in accounting and financial operation Management is also accustomed to manpower or personnel audits.

A complete marketing audit is something of an ideal or goal management to work toward. Rarely does a firm conduct an audit of the total components of its marketing mix and the interactions among the elements. The reason is that such an audit is too expensive and their consuming. Also, a total marketing-mix audit would be based to some extent upon data whose validity would be doubted by management.

Consequently it may be more reasonable first to conduct a complex analysis and investigation of the separate components of the marketing mix and to maximize the productivity and effectiveness of each of their elements before evaluating the interaction among them. With respect to field selling efforts, for example, such an approach to evaluation would involve an appraisal of the sales volume results, the related marketing expenses, and the performance of individual salesmen.

Often in individual firms there is a considerable amount of misdirect or misplaced marketing effort. Marketing efforts and cost follow the number of territories, customers, products, or other selling units, than the actual or potential sales volume or profit in these units.

The social aspects of marketing acquire importance

because markets directly involve either people or institutions in which decisions are made by people. The social structure of a market is influenced by interpersonal and intergroup relationships. The response of people to market stimuli is most properly analyzed in terms of demographic factors, psychological influences and the influences generated by society's culture and traditions. Thus when a market is said to have social influences, it means that the disciplines of sociology, psychology and cultural anthropology can be utilized to understand some of its phenomena. An examination of socio-psychological influences relevant to marketing affords insight into the consumer's behaviour in he market place.

Although the economic influences in marketing are many, the essential ones are (a) economic status of consumers, (b) kind of competition that permeates the market and (c) price determination.

Even though many influences in the market are not economic, the economic status of a society's people is the ingredient that turns desires into effective demand. Without income and money to spend, the socio-psychological aspects of an economy would be dormant. Money income remains the most fundamental basis for the functioning of the social variables and as such it gives impetus to other market influences.

Marketing is Political and Ethical Character: The political character of marketing lies in the legal nature of marketing activities which lead to exchange process. No business can operate very long without contact with the legal framework. Marketing functions within the framework of law. The legal dimension is one of the most highly formalized and complex influences on marketing behaviour. The ethical aspect of marketing has subtler impact than the legal framework. Law and ethics set boundaries of operation for marke ing.

Modern technology has wrought many changes in man and has profound effects on an economic system. It is the basis for today's production and distribution methods. Though the state of technology and its impact on marketing have seldom been a concern of marketing, technology becomes an integral force along with the others.

Scope of Marketing

The cope of marketing include all functions inherent in the marketing process. Marketing functions are as follows:

Marketing Functions

(i) Functions of Exchange

(a) Buying (b) Assembling (c) Selling

(ii) Functions of Physical Distribution

(a) Transportation (b) Inventory (c) Warehousing (d) Material Handling

(iii) Functions of Facilities

(a) Financing (b) Risktaking (c) After-sales Services

Exchanges Functions

Buying Functions: Buying functions have to be performed at various levels. A manufacturer has to buy raw materials, chemicals, etc. for production purpose. A wholesaler has to buy goods from manufactures for the purpose of sale to the retailers. A retailer has to sell goods to consumers.

Assembling Function: In assembling the manufacturer assembled goods purchased from various sources with a view to satisfying the needs of buyers.

Selling Function: Selling is the most important function for any company. Selling involves the transfer of ownership from the seller to the buyer. Goods are produced for selling them.

Physical Distribution

Transportation: Physical distribution consists of those marketing activities related to the physical handling of goods. Goods have to be transported from the end of production line to the consumer. Decision has to be taken on the efficient mode of transport.

Warehousing: Finished goods should be kept in the warehouse properly. Finished goods are packed, stored and dispatched to field warehouses which act as distribution centers.

Material Handling: It is necessary to select proper equipment for material handling.

Functions of Facilities

Financing: The importance of finance at reasonable rate of interest cannot be over emphasized. Arrangement for securing finance is very important for a marketer. There are various sources of finance like Commercial Banks, Government Agencies, Cooperative Banks, etc. The marketer must have a knowledge of the terms and conditions of credit facilities provided by different financial institutions.

Risk Taking: There are many risks which a marketer has to borne in the process of marketing goods and services. There are certain risks which can be insured against such as fire and accident risks. But there are other risks which cannot be insured, such as risks involved due to change in Government Policy or business cycle risks etc.

After Sales Service: These days the importance of after-sales facilities cannot be ignored by the marketer. The marketer has to plan for providing after-sale services, like repairs, replacements, etc.

3

New Dimensions of Modern Marketing

Historical Perspectives of Modern Marketing has taken on new dimensions through various management approaches. Marketing was defined as an exchange mechanism, in its early days and had been conceptualized as a function of selling. The efficacy of marketing was largely related with the personal salesmanship through advertising strategies for the consumer and industrial products. However, with the recognition of the difference between marketing and selling, the concepts turned more scientific and analytical. Marketing is now defined as a blend of behavioural and management science powered by creativity. Intuition, innovation, and inspiration tops them all. Marketing requires a scientific transformation in designing new products, identifying and recapitulating efficient channels and developing a powerful media exposure to set a challenging market environment. Thus, the application of scientific methods to marketing requires a high degree of conceptual clarity and the ability to translate it into action, coupled with innovative behaviour, besides a careful analysis of product-market environment. Marketing has also a philosophical dimension over the scientific consideration which explains the myth and reality of a business enterprise. It has been observed that business enterprises are likely to be more successful, when the business logistics, is guided by a strong marketing philosophy which responds to the following parameters:

(a) A close association with the customer,

(b) A value driven approach than a profit dynamic one,

(c) Product experimentation and

(d) Providing autonomy to enterprise.

Marketing therefore has two facets of business ethics and so also, ways for scientific transformation. It is essential to consider these issues in the management of business in a global perspective at the window of world trade prospects. Marketing is a complex phenomenon but can be understood in a simplified manner considering its integrative nature which broadens the scope. In the context o the consumer and industrial products, marketing may be understood as synonymous to the advertising and promoting function that primarily determines (i) the nature of a product (ii) the method of presentation in the market, (iii) promotional strategy and distribution style and (iv) the pricing approach.

The product presentation in the market is a scientific approach which includes the market and technology driven patters. Such product presentation approaches are found very close to the business philosophy aiming at improving the profit performance by identifying the need of each customer in the existing competitive environment.

Marketing has been defined in various dimensions with reference to profit and non-profit oriented organizations. On reviewing the different perspectives of marketing, there emerges four basic characteristics as under:

1. Profit orientation
2. Need-based marketing strategy
3. Product-market segmentation
4. Perfect placement o goods and services in the operational area, so that a competitive edge can be developed.

Product Presentation Patterns in Competitive Markets

Market-oriented

* Product application and economic benefits.
* Highlights the factor that influence customer's buying decision
* Promotes results of market research and R & D investment.
* Diagnosis and interprets the strategy, assumption, cost-structure and objectives of major components.

Technology-oriented

* comparative advantages among existing range of products.
* Cost-effective and low-maintenance profiles.
* Value-added technological product interpretation.
* Speaks about price performance, volume and business ratios.

Marketing has dynamic characteristics which are prone to change in reference to improved technology, fashion, market competition, cost factors and selling approaches. The focal characteristics of marketing keep changing in tune with the product, technology advancement and consumer response. It is found, that in the phases of economic development in a country, the marketing concepts change determining the domestic and international priorities. For instance, in the early post-independence period 1950-70s Sub-systems 1 & II) the business stress was on the farmers and agro-processed, products. Marketing efficiency increased in the following decade 1970-80s, prioritizing the industrial goods and consumer products, conceptualizing marketing function as 'diagnosis'. Later, the driving philosophy' of marketing is used as a dynamic string, leading the marketing revolution in the consumer goods and larger-scale industrial products. Another sub-system IV of marketing was developed during 1980-90s inculcating mechanised concepts in marketing through emphasis on electronic and export-oriented products. However, the out growth of intensive export-oriented approach has emerged in sub-system V moving through 1990-2000 Ad, which resulted in a trade liberalization concept to enhance the product markets at the window of the word. The conceptualisation of marketing logic in development perspective of the country. The reveals that the sub-systems in business environment are developed with the refinement in the functional concepts. These factors are also associated with the stages or growth of product marts—embryonic, premature, growth, nature and aging.

Thrust Areas in Marketing

The marketing of new products in developing countries, which allow a fee trade policy, is being performed under controlled conditions and donot possess any organized functioning pattern. The dynamism of product marketing largely moves round the business opportunities and strength thereof despite the competitive threats and indigenous weakness of the product. The status of marketing has been explained broadly as customer-oriented in oligopolistic conditions. Thus, an appropriate marketing planning for products in terms of trade channels, infrastructure, technology and behavioural dimensions needs to be emphasized for achieving better economic efficiency, besides, the management considerations of marketing-mix. However, prior to discussing marketing environment, it is essential to know the basic factors that contribute to the marketing management process in the competitive scenario.

The primary level conflicts in the marketing of products are related with the characteristics of economic environment and production. The lack of an effective coordination at various marketing programmes with the available resources, production process and the outlets is often found responsible for unfavourable instructions of the market forces. Many factors attributed to such conditions of a 'X' company. The marketing objectives of the company, could not be achieved for the following reasons.

1. Mismatch of consumer demand and product characteristics;
2. Lack of quality and innovative concept;
3. Absence of product orientation, product-line, branding and consumer awareness;
4. Inadequate communication skills and product promotional prospects; Competitive threat, higher dependency on private trade channel and lack of adequate institutional arrangements for production and marketing support.

It is to be understood in depth that products are competitive market-oriented and are sold in isolation. The products necessarily are subject to the reasonable demand generated by the existing customers as well as the potential segments. However, "meteoric' products appearing in the market do not aptly match with the consumer dead and quality and soon succumb to the market-forces. It is one of the reasons, that new products largely depend on the promotional agents and distributors who procure these products at a comparably premier price and market in dense transaction places take a higher degree of risk. Hence the marketing of products is a task, which needs to be performed scientifically. This concept weaves a net of alternative dynamics to operate simultaneously in the market to reduce the dependency of product marketing on one channel. The innovative characteristic is instrumental in marketing over the use of conventional methods which face the that of uncertainty, due to comparative advantages. Besides, there is a need to keep a constant watch over the market trend, by assessing the existing demand and consumer perceptions towards the products. Many market research studies have shown that the lack of proper product planning and assessment of potential consumers have drawn upon the major obstruction in product mobility in small towns. These attributes have been discussed in detail in the foregoing chapters. Broadly, it can be stated that the thrust areas of marketing attributes have a considerable role to play in building-p an effective marketing system. Thus there is a need to evolve an appropriate marketing mix in regard to identified products, considering the different economic and environmental factors.

Marketing is a customer-oriented process and it is essential to know who is the right customer and the needs thereof, The customer may be an individual, a firm or a country. This is particularly important in the marketing of industrial goods and services. The satisfaction of a customer is the prime concern in the marketing process and the entire ethos and shared values of the company owe the responsibility of satisfying the customer. Everyone in the firm, form top to bottom has a role to play in rendering maximum satisfaction to the customer. The holistic approach of the company in satisfying the customer should have the vision, mission and strategy, creativity, knowledge and shared values. The holistic approach for business firms is required for developing the organisation and promoting the marketing of the goods and services thereof. Peterson and Waterman had prescribed the concepts of 7Ss comprising systems, structure, strategy, style, staff, skills and shared values for effective organizational development. The marketing concept is based on the philosophy of customer satisfaction and to achieve this, the company has to look into its environment and work in total harmony with all the four satellite objectives. The behavioural dynamism should be the driving force behind all thee satellites. Knowledge enriches vision and helps in evolving a customer friendly mission of the company. This shows the way to harness innovative ideas by the using appropriate technology and management. However, the shared values and management styles of the company would help in disseminating knowledge and skills among the workforce of the company.

Market Environment

Identifying the customers' requirements is a major task for a marketing unction. All the input gathering activities of marketing are designed to know the needs of customers and the means of satisfying them, The consumers are the strength of the marketing company and they have varied preferences for goods and services. The basic responsibilities of the marketing function are identifying, anticipating and satisfying the customer requirements. In the changing business environment, the marketing function has the pressures from finance, manufacturing sector and human resource management. The finance marketing has to be oriented towards the demand of the consumers for buying and hiring of goods and services at reasonable interest rates. However, the finance markets should also look into the high consumer choice of the financial services and the competitive advantages. The manufacturing sector is facing the problems of rising costs, lower margins and splintered market. Under such circumstances, the marketing companies should building sustainable strategies than merely look for survival on the marginal gains. Hence the present business scenario demands for innovative strategies towards gaining the confidence of the consumers for proving their worth. The economic liberalization and increasing competition in the market place have replenished the concept of effective and sustainable marketing over mere sales and volume turnovers. It is essential to become the product or market leader by building the marketing relationship with the consumers. The consumer relationship should be more transparent and value-oriented. The companies should build the consumer strength, developing the management approaches on the following lines:

- Build a strong values system around internal customers
- Focus on individual needs of the consumers
- Disaggregate the value chain
- Encourage teamwork
- Develop genetic ideas between the processes
- Empower team and team members
- Transparency in each function
- Customize the goods and services process

- Redesign process to cut competition.

In developing the customer value, the company should consider both the customer needs – over or transparent and latent. The overt customer needs should be derived out of the existing wants of the customers and put on trial with the goods and services of the company. The customer experiences need to be analysed for developing the customer delight and the latent needs analysed should be explored through the focus group exercises.

The customer value may also be created through advertising and communication, effective distribution and sales, and high perceived use of value products and brands. The value chain development process. The customer delight may be established by measuring the direct contact with the customers, quality management, competitive advantages, developing customer sensitivity by giving them an opportunity to touch and feel, avoiding breach of understanding on either side and keeping continuous innovations. A good marketing firm should develop the following customer driven approaches for becoming the market leader.

The customer ma be categorized into five hierarchical categories—(in ascending order) committed buyer—who will also be spokesman for the brand, linkers of the brand—who are considered to be the brand friends, satisfied buyer with the hidden costs of brand switching, satisfied buyers of another category with no reasons to break-off relations. The last order customers may be categorized as switchers with no feeling for brand loyalty.

Components Marketing Management

Marketing Management is the process of product planning, pricing, promotion and distribution along with the services to generate transactions that satisfies the organisational and user objectives. The process involves need analysis, planning, execution and control mechanisms for promoting the product. It is a pattern of the marketing organisation which is carried out by the managers in the horizontal set-up and vertical hierarchy of personnel. Each job specifies a well-defined task and set of responsibilities such as market analysis, product design, sales, relationships, advertising and resource support to the users and intermediary marketing agents. The basic task of a marketing manager is to analyse, plan and execute the sales promotion programmes of the company. A balanced and logistic approach of a marketing manager will produce the desired level of achievement of targets and scope of market expansion. However, the populist image of a manager responsible for product marketing lies primarily in stimulating the demand for the product manufactured by them.

The marketing manager may face various types of demand and need for products to evolve stimulating strategies accordingly. The types of demand and characteristics thereof are exhibited in table. A saturated demand for the product is observed in an organisation when optimum satisfaction is endorsed by the consumers. The managerial approach requires to maintain the same state of demand in the long run too. However, if done so, supersaturtion of demand may occur which needs to be managed by effective distribution and consumer service approaches. The management of such market condition needs expert services for inventory management, distribution networking consumer service and analyzing the product response of consumers, besides quantitative and qualitative issues.

Sometimes, in the absence of an effective distribution network and consumer services, the demand for the product becomes irregular. This characteristic is also related with utility e.g., hospital equipments, public audio system equipments etc. in handing such demand irregularities, a flexible pricing and distribution approach ensuring the services may be the apt managerial approach. The concept of cost-effectiveness of goods and services transacted also plays an important role in setting a demand state. Thus, there always remains a latent demand for cost-effective goods and services viz.

Table 3.1: Demand States, Corresponding Characteristics and Managerial Approaches

Type of Demand	*Characteristics*	*Managers' Approach*
Saturated demand	* Achievement of all business targets.	* Maintenance of current Level of demand
	* Absolute satisfaction of consumers	* Continuous measurement of consumers' satisfaction.
Super-saturated demand	* Exceeding business targets * High sales * absolute sales factor of consumers.	* Effective product distribution. * Supply monitoring * Consumer service * Maintaining level of consumer satisfaction.
Irregular demand	* Seasonality in sales * Qualitative fluctuation * Changing marketing strategies * Supply gaps	* Attempt to regulate demand pattern through flexible pricing and product distribution approaches.
Latent demand	* strong consumer needs which remains unsatisfied for a long time.	* To measure the intensity of latent demand, market products accordingly.
Decreasing demand	* Falling consumer interest in specific products * Availability of substitutes * Increasing sales competition * Qualitative considerations.	* Creative marketing * Product relaunching strategies
Negative demand	* Non-serviceable goods * Unproductive services	* Buy-back policies * Improving product market relationship.
No demand	* Lack of awareness Indecisiveness of consumers.	* Launch the product afresh

Fuel efficient transport modes, strong and fire proof building materials etc. The latent demands can be managed by assessing the product-market potential for ingenuously developed products in view of the demand specifications. The marketing strategy should be applied if the demand for the products are decreasing, turning negative or at the edge of withdrawal. The product should be relaunched following the fundamentals in marketing management.

Components of Marketing Management

There are sequential steps in managing the marketing task of a product which moves through an integration path of a variety of components. Broadly, these components can be grouped into two major activities—(i) planning and (ii) implementation. Besides, the activities of market review considers the components of monitoring, strategy evaluation and opinion surveys. These components are synchronized order with major activities in marketing management. The demand analysis and identification of products matching to using demands is the first activity to be performed in market planning followed by the product positioning in planned market segment. The market segmentation needs to be done logically, considering the income brackets of the consumers. The planning for distribution network of products is also an important task which needs to be done for setting up an appropriate hierarchy of distributors viz., wholesale agents, authored retail dealers and local retailers. The market planning also consists of setting a business target and administering execution of marketing plans through an effective task allocation to the personnel of the company. The possibilities of business expansion should also draw attention in market planning exercise. The implementation strategy, is then to be drawn based on the draft of marketing plan. The issues of distribution management, competitive pricing, qualitative dimensions of product, market information system, advertising strategy and effective sales approach form the core of implementation strategy. It is essential to review the extent of consumer satisfaction, demand and business performance, following the designed marketing plan and implementation strategy. These exercises comprise the core of monitoring and evaluation activity in the overall marketing management process.

Activity Integration

Marketing Planning	Strategy implementation	Monitoring and evaluation
1. Demand analysis & product	1. Distribution Management	1. Consmer satisfaction review
2. Product Positioning	2. Pricing	2. Product demand review
3. Market segmentation	3. Quality control of products	3. Business performance
4. Districtuion network	4. Maintaining market information system	4. Marketing reforms.
5. Business targets and administration	6. Sales management and consumer service.	
6. Futre perspectives		

Figure 3.1: Integration path of activities in Marketing Management

Management Orientation

The nature of market, its demand and user expectations determine the kind of orientation required for marketing management. Broadly, there are two types of management orientations observed viz., (i) product-related and (ii) market-related. The market-related concept may further be classified into two kinds viz., (i) sales related and (ii0 marketing-related. However, such distinctions can be made theoretically, while in practice, the management observations are found to be same.

Product Concept

The production and product concepts are symbolic in marketing. The production is a process of manufacturing products of consumers' interest which have substantial utility and are available at a low cost. This is the traditionally guided principle for the managers of production-oriented companies for achieving high production and sales efficiency through a wide distribution coverage. The product concepts is a slightly improved variation over the production concept, which holds that the consumer will favour those products, which offer better quality, performance and feature. Such a motion has largely utility-oriented and qualitative dimensions.

Contemporary Lessons in Customerisation

Marketing delineate customerisation and it is essential for the marketing company to understand the needs of the customers about the goods and services across the regions. The customer leadership is also derived from the social and cultural behaviour besides the perceived use value and perceived price of the goods and services. There have been many experiments carried out by the national and multi-national companies in promoting customerism for their brands, goods and services, using various anchors of physical and behavioural nature.

Selling Concept

This is related with aggressive selling and promotion efforts of the organisational manager for stimulating consumers to buy the product. Selling cannot take place in isolation, where the consumer is left alone with the product, irrespective of interest and product quality. Thus, selling approaches need to be evolved in regard to product designing marketing planning, pricing, placement and promotion for effective results.

Marketing Concept

Marketing is a target-oriented approach, which hold the consumers supreme as the business target. It holds that the principle to achieve organisational goals lies in the consumers' satisfaction. So, the approach is oriented towards providing the best services to the consumers amidst the product competitors. The concept can be explained in the process of marketing planning, more practically for marketing managers. An effective marketing system can be formulated considering a number of stages in a synchronized way.

1. Identify needs and satisfying them
2. Make products which sells instead of trying to sell what is made.
3. Customer is supreme than product.
4. Liberty to customer in buying in terms of place, task, kind and quantity. Satisfying consumers esteem.
5. Draw marketing approach to get the consumer into confidence and achieve business targets.

The selling and marketing concepts are theoretically of a contradicting nature in terms of approach. However, both the activities are aimed at terminating the goal of earning profit.

The selling approach focuses on the products using sales promotion techniques in the market for achieving the profit goal of an organisation through an increased volume of sales. It can be stated that such an approach adopts the quantitative means to achieve the end results. On the contrary, the marketing concept is customer-oriented catering to their needs in turn with their satisfaction, within a given market environment. This concept focuses on satisfying the consumer needs through a coordinated approach of all eh marketing factors e.g. pricing, distribution, placement, promotion etc. however, the terminal goal of this concept also rests in profit-making through the parameter of customer satisfaction, unlike the selling concepts. Marking is also governed by some other factors related with environment and profitability. These are listed as under:

1. Market focus
2. Strategy coordination
3. Customer orientation
4. Profitability

The market focus determines the target customers, target product, organizational goals, financial targets, risk factors and profit target. The focus needs to be defined clearly to avoid ambiguities while the marketing strategies are in operation. To achieve this clarity, it is essential to ensure coordination along the various strategies drawn for pricing, distribution, promotion and customer service by the different groups of experts in the organisation. The coordination also needs to be set up among different class of personnel working in an organisation. As stated in the pretext. The customer orientation is the basic principle of marketing and needs to be exercised effectively. The ultimate goal of a business organisation is maximizing profit and minimizing risk, but certainly not at the cost of the customers' satisfaction.

Marketing as a field of study is generally categorized as being part of the broader field of business administration. However, marketing also involves considerations that extend beyond these boundaries. Marketing decisions are shaped by and influence the external environments of the firm. Marketing, therefore, has social, economic, legal, international, and political dimensions in addition to its managerial focus. Profitable solutions to marketing problems can only be realized if the significance of environmental change on the firm and its customers is recognized. These external forces which affect consumer behaviour and business action must be reflected in marketing policies, plans, programmes, and decisions.

The student of marketing must develop a facility for integrating useful contributions from many disciplines. He must also understand the functional purpose of each component in a marketing action system. Illustration I depicts a total marketing system and services as a model for the study of marketing management. The conceptual relationships portrayed are developed in subsequent illustrations and readings. This marketing systems model is presented in the spirit of the following passage from Konrad Lorenz:[1]

I am aware that the task I have set myself makes excessive demands upon my pen. It is almost impossible to portray in words the functioning of a system in which every part is related to every other in such a way that each has a causal influence on the others. Even if one is only trying to explain a gasoline engine it is hard to know where to begin, because the person to whom one seeks to explain it can only understand the nature of the crankshaft if he has first grasped that of the connecting rods, the pistons, the valves, the camshaft, and so on. Unless one understands the elements of a complete system as a whole, one cannot understand them at all. The more complex the structure of a system is, the greater this difficulty becomes—and it must be surmounted both in one's research and in one's teaching. Unfortunately the working structure of the instinctive and culturally acquired patterns of behaviour which make up the social life of man seems to be one of the most complicated systems we know on this earth.

The External Environments of Marketing

Marketing managers, by the nature of their problems, are environmentalists. They give attention to the implications of environmental changes for marketing policies and practices. Illustration I shows the external environment in which the systemic functions of marketing are managed. These environments and interactions affect marketing opportunities, customer behaviour and satisfaction, and the degree of success achieved by the business.

In this model, the major external environmental influences on business actions are categorized as: scientific and technological forces; life style and life space forces; ethical, legal, and social forces; and both domestic and international economic and political forces. Each of these forces interacts with the corporate system. Their impact on marketing management is investigated in further chapters.

The marketing manager needs to appreciate the pervasive influence of these forces on consumer attitudes and behaviour. While the activities of any single business cannot appreciably alter any of the external forces, the converse relationship exists—any one force can affect business outcome. Customers react to and help shape their environments, and market opportunities or problems result from changed customer attitudes toward products and services.

Three linkage levels involved in the analysis of marketing systems are shown in the model.

1. Marketing activities are linked through the corporate enterprise system to the various public and private agencies external to the firm. Examples of these agencies, which are not depicted in the model, include: suppliers; advertising firms and media; financial institutions; governmental and private research organisations; federal, state, and local governmental commissions; transportation companies; and the various publics.

2. Linkages exist between marketing and the other business functions that comprise the corporate enterprise system. These other areas are represented by the firm's human, physical, and financial resources, its competitive structure, and its goals. Because the purpose of this model is depiction of a marketing action system, other functional areas of the business have not been explicitly differentiated. Similar models could be constructed for production, finance, and other functions of an enterprise.

3. The systemic functions of marketing are linked to produce an effective marketing-customer satisfactions mix. Three sub-mixes—product-services, communications, and distribution—are combined to achieve marketing objectives. The objective of the marketing mix is to balance marketing objectives. The objective of the marketing mix is to balance marketing effort with marketing opportunity in order to provide optimal marketing support of stated corporate goals.

The nature of marketing operations within the corporate enterprise system, and emphasizes that corporate goals are achieved by concentrating on defined areas of market opportunity or, more precisely, on customers in particular market segments. Corporate goal setting is recognized today as a complex process for conglomerate, multinational, multi-plant firms.

The Consumer

Chapter three deals with the consumer, the focal point of marketing effort. The consumer, by his decision to buy or not buy a product, holds veto power over the firm's entire marketing and business effort. Many of the elements that influence consumer behaviour and satisfaction are considered in this chapter.

Like the others, Chapter three is future-oriented. One purpose of analyzing the articles in the book is to enable the reader to better understand and ultimately meet the problems consumers will have in the future. For example, understanding of consumer behaviour is increased by studying trends in life style and life space forces. In Chapter three, some of these trends are identified, and their impact on marketing programmes are treated in detail.

Market segmentation provides one way of identifying marketing opportunities that have arisen because of changing life styles. Broad potential markets are broken down into many smaller segments, each with its own tastes, preferences, values, and needs.

The market segmentation concept is the basis of a marketing strategy directed toward consumers with particular life styles and needs. While demographic methods are basic, other criteria for market segmentation are also useful. Examples of newer methods of segmentation analysis include the determination of differences in buyer attitudes, motivations, values, patterns of usage, and aesthetic preferences.

Consumer motivation is a function of the extent to which human needs are satisfied. One theory of human motivation holds that needs are satisfied. One theory of human motivation holds that needs are arranged on a continuum that ranges from basic physiological needs to those of self-actualisation.[2] An appreciable measure of satisfaction of lower needs is a precondition for emergence of higher ones. The marketing manager's task to is to assemble a market offer that promises gratification of at least one level in this hierarchy of needs.

Consumer behaviour is influenced by the life style ad life space force discussed in this book. Many marketing efforts of American business and many of the changes taking place in consumption cannot be understood unless life style trends are considered.

There seems to be an increasing worldwide interest in personal achievement, social goals, and a better way of life. This has been described as the "revolution of rising expectations" and seems to be worldwide. For example, throughout the world there is an upward mobility thrust toward more education and more real income. The above trends are especially evident in the United States. Trends toward home entertainment and family-centered enjoyment are related to increasing discretionary time and mobility. Changes in the geographic distribution of the population are reflected in a redistribution of the labour force and purchasing power.

Tomorrow's customers may have problems that are quite unlike the buying and consumption problems prevalent today. Future consumers will generally be better educated, have greater mobility, possess more discretionary income, and have more time to spend that income. Hopefully, new communication and distribution patterns will lead to increasingly informed decisions and prompt satisfaction of consumer wants.

Decision Making in Marketing

The articles in Chapter four deal with marketing as a prime focus of managerial decision making. Marketing management is becoming increasingly analytical as models and techniques for information gathering and problem solving are developed, and as new marketing applications of existing scientific methods are discovered. Scientific and technological developments are having a continuing impact on the advancement of science in marketing. For example, the computer is exerting a significant influence on such areas as marketing planning, the evaluation of promotional alternatives, and distribution systems. Some authorities see marketing as the great growth area of computer applications in business. The rapid accumulation of new knowledge is resulting in widespread application of mathematical, statistical, economic, psychological, and sociological techniques to marketing problems. These interdisciplinary contributions to marketing promise better understanding of complex consumer needs and of other marketing problems.

Marketing Management Functions

The functions of marketing management identified in the upper center discussed in further chapters. The functions are marketing opportunity assessment, marketing planning and programming, marketing organization and leadership, and evaluating and adjusting marketing effort. The marketing management team must perform these four entrepreneurial functions if the firm is to develop an efficient corporate marketing system in a changing environment.

Marketing opportunity assessment centers on the delineation of actual and potential customers and their wants and needs. Market opportunity exists when a business either possesses or can develop capabilities that enable it to profitably satisfy the wants of potential customers. The business must continually develop marketing strategies that will enable I to cultivate these market opportunities.

Research and development activities of business, government, and educational institutions are resulting in increasing numbers of new consumer and industrial products. Similarly, increased productivity resulting from automation and other forces has resulted in production capacity that enables most manufacturing firms to produce more than they can sell. The mass production capability of American industry is predicated on the discovery of new markets and the expansion of existing ones. This is one of the factors underlying the marketing orientation of American business.

Planning is essential to the organization, operation, and control of a business. Planning also provides a basis for an integrated systems orientation and a coordinated marketing strategy. The development of new products and new markets raises organizational and leadership problems for marketing management. The interaction that occurs between an organisation and its environment illustrates the dynamics of the systems approach and reflects the demands being placed on the marketing organization and its leadership.

Evaluating and adjusting the marketing effort enables the firm to react to changes occurring in the environment. The process of change—and the ability to cope with it –is a major challenge to marketing management. Financial and integrative controls are used to keep the marketing effort keyed to areas of profitable market opportunity.

Managing the Marketing Mix

The lower central section provide an overview of the dimensions and complexities of developing and managing a marketing mix. Preparing an effective marketing mix that furthers attainment of corporate objectives is the marketing manager's responsibility.

A marketing mix consists of three sub mixes—the product and service mix, the communications mix, and the distribution mix. The product and services mix is composed of elements that form the set of utilities a customer buys. Examples of utility set contents include the product, price, services, container, brand, label information, conditions of sale, and warranty. A communications mix consists of the firm's efforts to disseminate information about its market offer to the potential byrs. The elements of a communications mix are advertising, sales promotion, personal selling, merchandising, and special sales aids. The distribution mix I formed of two major components—channels of distribution through which goods and titles to goods flow from the firm to the ultimate purchasers, and physical distribution, which is concerned with loading, transporting, storing, and delivering the product.

The marketing manager's responsibility for formulating an effective mix and for putting it into practice does not culminate with the sale of the product or service. He must not neglect the post-transactional ingredients of his marketing mix if the firm's long-range marketing strategy is to be successful.

International Marketing

The external environmental areas of domestic and international economic and political forces. The evolution of international markets is one of the most significant trends in contemporary marketing. Further chapters presents an international view of marketing and the development of the multinational firm.

Many of the forces described in the book are related to the United States market. However, their impact in the United States Portends changes of a similar nature in many countries throughout the world. For example, the knowledge explosion, particularly in science and technology, is influencing nearly all cultures. New marketing opportunities are presented by widespread rising consumption expectations and increased interest in personal achievement and social gains. Political unrest in newly formed nations around the world reflects, at lest in part, dissatisfaction with present living standards. These people want, and intend to obtain for themselves, those goods now enjoyed by consumers in more advanced economies. Similarly, some nations with controlled economies seem to be moving from a production to a partial consumer orientation. The marketing knowledge and ability possessed by multinational firms can aid immensely in the development of balanced economies in both new and changing political-economic systems. Marketing managers must recognize, analyze, and adjust to the marketing systems of each international market. Attempts to improve the efficiency of these marketing systems must be based on a thorough evaluation of the system's socio-political environment.

Marketing plays a key role in the economic growth of developing countries. To the extent that the socioeconomic growth of a nation is related to the marketing process, marketing can be a critical element in the development process. Marketing is not only an economic tool, but a political and social tool as well. Ultimately, marketing's most important social role may lie in its contribution to the stimulation and facilitation of world peace.

Interdisciplinary Dimensions of Marketing

Marketing practitioners and academicians realize that various ethical, legal, social, economic, and political forces are becoming increasingly important for marketing Illustration I identifies these forces as major influences on markets. Their effects on marketing thought and action are discussed in this book.

The socioeconomic dimensions of marketing account, in part, for the growing concern of business and marketing leaders with public and private views of social responsibility in business. Te continuing emphasis on the need for businesses to increase their efforts to fulfill their assigned citizenship roles reflects an expanding concept of business' social responsibility.

In order to fully understand marketing's dynamics and the changes in marketing described in this book, students and managers must not only understand problem-solving techniques, they must also understand the theory underlying these techniques and practices. Some developments that influence marketing as a discipline, the interdisciplinary approach to marketing, and the contributions of theory to marketing management are explored in this book.

The articles included in the book were chosen for their contribution to an understanding of managerial marketing. The perspective throughout is that marketing managers must equip themselves to better understand the problems of potential customers and, ultimately, to help customers satisfy their requirements in a manner that meets the needs not only of customer and firm but also of society.

Marketing System Defined

The marketing management philosophy is based on a systems perspective of decision-making. The systems approach to marketing has already had a substantial impact on the development of marketing thought and the management of marketing activity. This approach provides a conceptual framework for market planning, determination of the marketing mix, physical distribution, and the use of operations research techniques in marketing. Systems thinking recognizes the interrelations and inter-connections among the components of a marketing system.

The systems approach is based n the work of Von Bertalanffy, who is credited with coining the phrase "general systems theory." He defined a system as a set of objects together with the relationships among them and their attributes.

Marketing institutions and operations can be perceived as complex, large-scale systems. For analytical purposes any group of marketing elements and activities that can be physically or conceptually delineated is a marketing system. A system is a collection of entities that can be understood as forming a coherent group. The fact that the entities can be defined as a coherent group is what differentiates a system from a meaningless collection of parts.

In marketing systems, there are flows of products, services, money, equipment, and information. It is these flows that largely determine the survival and growth capacities of a firm. The systems approach places great emphasis on the analysis of flows and communications. It stresses the development of communication systems for transmitting information about changing market environments and subsequent adjustments of marketing policies and strategies.

Elements of Marketing Systems

Marketing systems include the following components:

1. A set of functionally interdependent marketing relationship among people and institutions in the system—manufacturers, wholesalers, retailers, facilitating agencies, and consumers.

2. Interaction between individuals and firms to maintain relationships, and facilitate adjustment to change, innovation, cooperation, and competition.

3. Establishment of objectives, goals, targets, beliefs, symbols, and sentiments that evolve from and reinforce the interaction, thus producing realistic marketing objectives and programmes, and creating favorable images, attitudes, and opinions.

4. A consumer-oriented environment within which interactions take place, subject to the constraints of a competitive market economy, the legal and socioeconomic environment, and the evolving relationships and methods of marketing entities.

5. Technology of marketing, including communications media, credit facilities, standardization and grading, marketing research, and physical distribution.

Kinds of Marketing Systems

The operational delineation of a system depends, in part, on the dominant activity being described, i.e., whether it is a sales management system, a manufacturer-dealer system, a physical distribution system or a corporate communications system. But the systems perspective is a useful one regardless of the kind of system being delineated, since it directs analysis to the actions and reactions of the firm as it operate within its many environments.

Marketing systems maybe of two types—conceptual or physical. Most marketing systems are conceptual. However, some systems, such as physical distribution systems, are physical entities. Also, the parts of a marketing system may be within or outside the formal boundaries of the firm. Many of them extend beyond the firm. For example, a manufacturer's marketing system may well include wholesalers, retailers, financial institutions, and advertising agencies.

A marketing system as an assemblage or combination of activities, institutions, ad operations is composed of subsystems. Any marketing institutions, and operation sis composed of subsystems. Any marketing component can be explained in term of various systems. Hierarchies of subsystems exist. Marketing systems are linked to larger formal systems. The advertising department can be viewed as system, as can the marketing department, the business enterprise, or the totality of a number of business enterprises.

Marketing systems may be perceived of as small systems, middle-range systems, and large systems[3] Small systems are concerned with marketing within the firm. The marketing mix or the physical distribution system are examples. The middle-range systems are those concerned with marketing's linkage to other functional activities, such as finance and production. A good example is the credit system. The large system or macro-system is concerned with marketing's linkages among manufacturers, or manufacturers, wholesalers, and retailers. Voluntary cooperatives are large systems.

A question can be raised about the appropriate structural forms that marketing systems should take. The true test is survival and effectiveness. Certain forms and system structures are more suitable at one period of time in a market than at another. Over time, the elements of the system that are approved by the marketplace are the most appropriate.

4

Strategies of Customer and Producer Mix Under Competition

Marketing is an integrated effort of various attributes linked wit the corporate objective of the organisation. The environment which encompasses the marketing activity is volatile and keeps changing in reference to the business policy of the competing firms, fashion, legal interventions and innovations. Thus, in the modern era, most of the companies put growing efforts on organising their marketing avenues in response to significant changes in the market. In this process, it is essential to know the consumer orientation at the very beginning. The research and development wing of the company need to attend on the new ideas and engineer tem to manufacture the products desired by the consumers. Some of the essential determinants in the process are:

- Consumer feedback
- Product improvement
- Distribution and purchase
- Marketing set-up
- Zero defects

In a marketing organization, there should be a continuous

flow of information from the consumers which encourages the learning process for the manufacture to improve the product. The ideas generated through the feedback of consumers need to be evaluated in order to accelerate the product improvement process. However, the company should develop a proper match with the supply and distribution system to ensure the availability of the products to the consumers.

Organising Market

The marketing department in an organization should consist of a chain of functionaries for managing the various marketing operations such as consumer survey, production, research and development, distribution, pricing, marketing finance, sales, promotion, administration and the like. The functionaries should have a horizontal and vertical network to perform their tass efficiently and provide feedback to the decision managers. The horizontal networking needs to be done for promoting product distribution, sales and promotion at the grassroots level. It is advised to spread geographically covering all the marketing sensitive points of the hinter and of the operation of the company.

The service functions have to be coordinated, monitored and evaluated at the middle management level, whereas the planning functions need to be taken care of by the top management of the organisation. The service functions include the administration of sales personnel, promotion, marketing research and market surveys. Functions pertaining to strategic planning, product planning, marketing research and decisions about the new projects comprising the planning and programme functions rests with the top management. The area functionary in a marketing organization should provide a regular feedback to the middle management to enable them to evaluated the performance and modify the marketing strategies as and when required. The product Manager's role is to develop the product pans and administer them in the selected market segments. Other important functions which include the job chart of product manager are:

- Formulation of sustainable an competitive product plans
- Formulating annual operational marketing plans
- Forecasting sales
- Planning sales force
- Developing sales promotion strategies
- Managing the market information system
- Analyzing marketing problems, consumer grievances and working out suitable solutions for them.
- Suggesting product improvement.

The responsibilities of the product managers cannot be numbered, as the list is not exhaustive. The product manager has to interact with different types of interest groups in order to ensure a smooth functioning of a marketing organisation. On the product front, the interactions f the product managers are markedly with the personnel of research and development, production, distribution, promotion, media, and consumer services.

The operational control in a marketing organisation comprise the streamling of sales, distribution, promotion and product innovation activities. The sales control may be administered by scrutinizing the new contracts, competitive sales approaches and new proposals of expanding the sales avenues. It is essential to identify brand loyalty among the distributors and encourage the exclusive distribution for effective monitoring of sales of the company's product. Promotional control consists of administering of effective communication strategies to the distributors and consumers by way of advertisement, consumer surveys and sales campaigns. Periodical reviews need to be done by the operational control personnel of a company in order to build up an image of the company and products thereof in the market. One of the important tasks of operational control is streamlining the consumer services. This activity can be performed knowing fully the perceptions of the consumers about the services offered by the company through bench-marketing. This technique enables one to see at a glance the performance of services and further investment in the consumers services providing the value in their perceptions.

The marketing manager of a company may prepare a consumer service matrix denoting high, medium and low perceptions of different segments of consumers and identify the target area.

It is expected that the marketing manager should initiate clear actions, if the elements of consumer service fall into this part of the matrix. The target area emphasizes the importance to be given to the consumers of the "target" Segment.

In a vertical organisational network, often the problem of striking a balance of the operational decisions between the apex and lower level functionaries occur. The operational decisions consists of marketing and non-marketing functions. The marketing function consists of planning programme, implementation monitoring and evaluation while the non-marketing functions consists of research and development and public relations. The balance need to be struck as to what mix of these activities will be attended by apex and grassroots level functionaries. An important point to remember is that with the functional decentralization, there remain changes of duplication of effort and in such circumstances, networking decisions have to be taken on the basis of the extent of expenditure on performing the tasks. However, there exist advantages and disadvantages of functional centralization or otherwise. Some of the main considerations for organising marketing are:

* Lines of authority and tasks should not be ambiguous but clearly stated to the functionaries at various levels.

* The structure for marketing organisation must be

acceptable, conducive and dynamic to perform the functions on time and well informed.

* All the sub-activities should be properly coordinated.

* Information on marketing activities need to be collected by an efficient department of the organisation and the relevant facts need to be made available to all the functional units to set their strategies.

* It is essential to maintain integrity among the marketing personnel in an organisation.

Customer and producer mix

Alike customer matrix the produce matrix also needs to be constructed for developing the competitive strategy. In this process the matrix may e plotted using the information on the marketing effectiveness of the company and the unit cost of the products on the x and Y axis respectively. The effectiveness of the firm may be identified on the basis of operational competence and system competence. The operational competence refers to the technical competence including production, packaging, distribution, quality control and information management. The cost efficiency largely depends on the technical competence of the company. The system competence includes vale assurance, value enhancement and innovation. The competitive strategy for the mass market it is necessary to improve the effectiveness and lower the unit cost of the product. The company may move its position of the product to the quadrant where the performance of the company as well as the unit cost also remains high due to improved technological intervention and marketing interventions. However, in a situation where the unit cost of the product and performance of the organisations both are low, the growth rte would slow down and the strategies need to be built upto revive the growth first and then by sustaining the competition. In case of high unit cost of the product and low performance of the organisation, none of the competitive strategies would prove worth due to non-validity of economy of scale. The company has to make mainly decision on either diversify its activities of paying more concentration for strengthening its market bases. In this decision process the company has to consider some of the important variables like spill over effects in terms of supply backlog, product improvement, packaging, price sensitivity and operational problems including cost of distribution and margin spread. The company should also took into the market performance of product, effective consumer response in terms of sales and the convenience of the consumers in terms of access to the product.

The company may follow the checklist of activities in building the competitive strategy as stated below:

- Scanning of the environment
- Identifying relevant economic inevitable and rigid factors Identifying the key trends of major competing brands
- Political, economic, socio-cultural and technological factors affecting the product market
- Conduct an activity cost analysis for the upstream ad downstream linkages wit the company
- Identify the core competence of the company
- Look into the data bank of the company's operational and human resource variables
- Mission and key strategies
- Culture and leadership style.
- Competitive position
- Adjustment and acquaintance with the government policies
- Determine levels of cost in the production and operations
- Price levels and consumer segments,

Strength of demand for the product Opportunities for expansion of product-line and market

Prepare contingency plans of marketing.

The process of building competitive strategy takes substantial time ad needs to be attended through the careful analysis. It is essential that the action required to start implementation of the selected strategy needs to be prioritized and documented.

The Formulation of a Market Strategy

Business management has been called many things: it commonly is described as an art; some describe it as a guessing game. Perhaps the height of wisdom on his subject is contained in the phrase, "business is business," for business is not like anything else. Clearly, success as a business executive requires what some people describe as "artistry" and intuition—though these probably are far less vital than just plain luck. In addition, in this paper endeavours to prove, successful business management demands careful and maximum application of the scientific method.

The scientific method obviously needs no defense; only an eccentric will maintain that guesses are more valid bases for decision than careful observation and experimentation. However, the phases of business management that are amenable to scientific methods are far from obvious. Little is to be gained by pointing a finger at businessmen for having managerial decision-making in a relatively primitive state until recently while production men applied the fruits of science to achieve miracles in the factory. The very large number of business failures and high turnover among business executives have been punishment enough. However, the contrast between the methods by which managerial and production decisions are made deserves emphasis, for there exists an influential body of executives—and some academicians—who find the main ingredient of business success to be "good judgement and practice of the managerial art." These phrases are question begging unless one is able to define what is meant by good judgment and the managerial art. Moreover, such as view deprecates the importance of fact-gathering, rigorous reasoning, hypothesis-testing—and all elements of the scientific method that can be applied to many of the problems faced by businessmen.

It may appear pretentious to link business management with the scientific method. When one speaks of "scientific management" or "scientific marketing" he simply means that business decisions should have the maximum benefit of factual support, close rigorous reasoning, and empirical test; also, that every conclusion reached should be open to challenge and be capable of rational defense. There is no room in this concept for bowing to authority, deference to the intuitions or experience" of older men or persons associated with the business for a longer time; it requires that decisions be made on the basis of facts and logical argument rather than by appeal to authority.

No one familiar with business dreams that it will become an "exact science" which rest upon a body of proved principles analogous to what has been produced by the chemist and physicist. Everyone knows that duplicable experiments cannot be the main technique employed for arriving at generalizations applicable to business. The methods available to business executives for solving concrete problems are, at bet, relatively crude, unreliable and unproved by the standards of most physical sciences. However, the year vastly more reliable than reliance on hunch, intuitions, feel and guesses, or appeal to authority.

The scientific method, or the most scientific techniques applicable to business—however one prefers to express it—is not to be confused with the use of the conference or committee method of decision-making. All too often, these methods are applied in a manner that brings several uninformed people together to pool their thoughts and hammer out a common agreement. A "bull session," no matte by what elegant title it may be dignified, will not produce valuable results unless at least some participant are very well informed.

Once maximum use is made of observation and experimentation, discussion will generally prove very valuable; however, it certainly cannot substitute for the collection and analysis of facts.

Practitioners in most fields—especially those who practice for a fee—understandably are anxious to persuade others that their fields of specialization are sciences. Only recently, however, have some person specializing are sciences. Only recently, however, have some persons specializing in business fields claimed to be "applied" scientists. To understand that they claim, one must also know what they disavow. Almost all admit their inability to remotely approach the accuracy, predictability and even objectivity of most physical sciences. But they maintain that there do exist data, methods of data collection, experimental and testing procedures, and methods of analyzing and testing findings whose application to business would greatly increase the proportion of correct managerial decisions. Rather than great accuracy in absolute terms, these people claim to be relatively accurate in a field where attempts at systematic and rigorous answers to problems remain exceptional.

How can Business Management be made more Scientific?

To make business management into an applied science, executives, must first clarify their firm's objectives. Although the selection of ultimate business objectives is necessarily unscientific, for they express the fundamental values f individuals who establish broad policy, operating objectives stated fully, clearly, and concretely are indispensable if one is to make managerial decision-making amenable to the scientific method. Once objectives are known, the selection of means becomes the task of appraising, by the best means available, the relative effectiveness of alternatives.

A Statement of a Firm's Broad Objectives. Business objectives can be stated on a variety of levels; one must begin with the ultimate—the broadest and most general—and work back to the more narrow and specific ends that they imply. The two most widely expressed ultimate objectives of corporate management these days are: first, to make maximum profits for the firm over the life of the enterprise and strictly within the limits of the law; and, second, to conduct operations in a manner that gives equal weight to the claims of; stockholders, labour, consumers and government. Both of these broad objectives must be translated into more specific market goals if they are to be very helpful to executives responsible for making concrete business decisions.

Statement of Market Objectives. In pursuit of maximum profits, for example, management might set its operating objectives at: a maximum of dollar or unit sales; a maximum share of total or of particular geographic markets; maximum profit figured as a percentage of net worth or of sales; it might set itself the objective of a steadily increasing return on sales or profits; or the goal of an increasing market share. Bt even if narrowed this far, the objectives are not as helpful as they can be made. It is possible to state market objectives in a form that facilitates an application of the scientific method.

Market objectives are best expressed as customer types—narrowly defined—whose patronage the business will try especially to win. (Of course, it will not turn away others desiring to buy.) Once objectives have been refined to this on, management is in a position to formulate more specific problems in a manner that makes it readily amenable to solution by the scientific method:

A determination of the types of customers the firm should try to service in particular does not flow simply and logically from a firm's ultimate objectives. A careful consideration of alternative markets must underline the selection of those markets to be cultivated intensively.

Concept of a "Market Strategy"

Put differently, use of "scientific" methods for making marketing decisions calls for what is here termed a "market strategy," The main purpose of this paper is to explain what a market strategy consists of and how it can serve as a potent organizing tool for the decisions of business executives. It may well assist students of marketing by giving a central structure to various facets of the study of business.

A markct strategy consists of two parts: (1) the definition of market targets—selecting the types of customers whose patronage will be sought; and (2) the "composition of a marketing mix"—picking a combination of sales promotion devices that will be employed. Market targets represent the operating objectives (which are subject to change of curse) of top management; the marketing mix represents a combination of instruments by which these objectives are pursued.

The scientific method finds its greatest potential application to marketing by calling for a rigorous appraisal of the relative effectiveness of alternative means of winning the patronage of particular types of potential customers. The scientific marketer must assemble the best evidence available, determine what additional evidence should be gathered, subject all information collected to rigorous analysis, formulate and test hypotheses regarding the effect on unit sales of such things as: price changes, changes in the quality of the product, advertising outlays, number of salesmen, margins offered retailers, number of retail outlets, etc.

It will be acknowledged at the outset that no generalizations about these matters can be applied to all or even to many products. Answers to specific marketing problems probably differ for each individual business—and will not even be stable for it over long periods of time. Thus, top management must reconcile itself to an unending study of the relative effectiveness of sales promotion devices. An agreement's success in achieving the market a targets it sets itself will, it is maintained here, depend upon the scientific rigor with which it conducts this endless study—rather than upon the artistry and intuition of its top executives.

The steps involved in the formulation of a market strategy will be discussed in broad general terms in this paper. First, the determination of market targets will be taken up; thereupon, the composition of a marketing mix will be discussed.

Definition of Market Targets. No one can hope to please everybody! Person who attempt to win the friendship of everyone are likely to have few friends, for they will lack individuality and basic personality.

Many will doubt their sincerity and almost everyone will get an uneasy feeling in their presence and think that there is something "fishy" about them. Businesses who try to sell to everybody risk a similar fate. If they attempt to convince their prestige conscious customers that their product represents the highest possible quality and the brand that customers buy if they do not have to worry about cost, they may repel potential customers who are extremely concerned about economy But, if they claim that the product represents both the highest possible quality and the lower price, they will be believed by almost no one.

No business needs to sell to all potential customers. A fraction of the total market is all any firm need hope for— and the Department of Justice frowns on those wit more ambitious hopes. IT IS Almost always wise for a management to select consciously the types of customers it will try to win as their firm's main patrons; in so doing, management can mobilize the full resources of the firm to a clearly defined task. To make such a selection, management should first divide the total potential market into its "significant segments.

Potential customers must be divided into groups that have some significance from the standpoint of what management can and should do about them. The most important criteria for segmenting the market for any product are: (1) strength of their need or desire for the product: (2) channels (media, distribution outlet, etc.) through which they can be reached; (3) "appeals" (lines of argument) to which they are responsive; (4) degrees of responsiveness to particular types of sales appear (that is, their ability to be influenced by price considerations, availability of credit, sales talk of salesmen, etc.); and (5) physical location.

The most significant market segments vary widely from product to product. Customers must be classified according to the many special features of the product in question and of the circumstances under which it is sold. In almost every case, however, there are two types of criteria that should be employed: the first are the features traditionally used by market analysts. These generally can be measured and include such things as: incomes, marital status, size of family, religion age, size of community, whether or not the product is already owned, the age and condition of the product owned, etc. The second are social and psychological characteristics that almost always are unmeasurable and apply particularly to the product in question. For example, one might divide potential customers of most products into: the self-confident and those who are unsure of themselves; the adventurous and those craving the familiar; the ostentatious and the modest, etc. In addition, particular attitudes are confronted in the marketing of some products but have no being upon others. For example, it seems to have been established that the use of instant coffee is associated in the minds of many housewives with neglect of a wife's proper duties. This attitude is not likely to have any bearing upon the sale of women's hats, however.

As already indicated, the criteria by which potential customers are divided should meet two tests; (1) they should reflect differences which indicate or affect the actions that businessmen should take in trying to win their patronage; and (2) they should apply to the particular product in the specific markets in which they are being sold. In classifying potential customers, one should err, if at all, in the direction of dividing them into too many rather than too few groups. Both measurable and unmeasurable characteristics should be combined into one scheme of classification. It is likely that one will end up with many scores of market segments; as stated the more the better.

Those segments should then be scrutinized carefully to determine; (1) which ones are least adequately served at present: (2) those which the particular firm is best qualified to attract—because of its product, personnel, tradition, reputation, standing in the customer's mind, etc.; and (3) those that management would like to make the core of the business over the future, simply on grounds of personal taste.

By scrutinizing the total potential market broken down into segments possessing significance for action, a management may well find that several parts of the market had gone relatively uncovered. It so, it may profit by cultivating those particular markets, using measures especially effective in winning their patronage.

Management should also select the market segments to cultivate intensively by matching its own resources against what is needed to "sell" particular types of prospective customers. Special qualities about a firm's management, location, past performance, design of product. Company tradition, etc. may make it particularly effective in serving certain market segments. To match the firm against market segments involves a realistic appraisal of the firm's strengths and weakness and of the factors that influence the purchase of each potential customer group. Often a firm will find itself especially suited to win patronage from particular types of customers—which may also be actively cultivated by some of its competitors. Not infrequently, there is a conflict between market targets that are an covered and those for which the firm has special talent. A choice must be made, and often it will not be an easy one.

Businessmen are people! They have likes and dislikes that do and should influence their decisions. The most profitable markets may be found in regions which require location in uncomfortable climates or uncongenial social environments. In part, a selection of market segments for intensive cultivation must be influenced by such considerations. However, management cannot long follow its inclinations if they would result in persistent losses.

To summarize what has been said upto this point, a scientific market strategy first requires that a business formulate general and broad objectives. These must then be translated into operating objectives, by specifying the particular market segments the firm will cultivate most intensively.

To make such a decision, which is among he most crucial that management must make, requires an exhaustive division of all potential customers into segments which possess marketing significance—that is, they are best cultivated in different ways. The selection of the particular segments that the firm should cultivate intensively should be made on grounds of the extent to which they are being neglected at present, the special qualifications that the firm possesses to serve them and the taste of the business owners.

Composition of the Marketing Mix. Once the firm's market targets have been specified, management faces the task of selecting measures most likely to achieve them. In modern marketing parlance, we must discuss the "marketing mix."

The "marketing mix" is composed of large battery of devices which might be employed to induce customers to buy a particular product. The same devises are involved whether one is of thinking of inducing altogether new buyers to purchase the product or of shifting customers from rival bands to one's own. These devices are here termed" sales promotion devices "and include a wide variety of instruments. It is wise to list separately those which are at the disposal of manufactures and those which may be employed by distributors and dealers.

Sales promotion devices that might be used by manufactures to induce customers to buy their products include such things as: quality of product, special product features, amount of advertising outlays, lines of advertising outlays, lines of advertising appeals employed, types of advertising media used, number of personal salesmen employed, quality f salesmen, distributive channels employed, quality of distributors used, number of distributions, location of sales effort (geographically), product guarantees, servicing arrangements, credit and accommodations supplied.

Distributors and dealers might use the following instruments to induce customers to patronize them; price inducements, advertising, number and quality of salesmen, location, air conditioning, location of merchandise departments in the store, breadth of selection offered customers, width of aisles, hours of operation, return privileges, credit accommodation, delivery service, etc.

Even though the foregoing lists of sales promotion devices are far from complete, they are long. And, what is especially significant, management must make decisions regarding almost every one of them. Either consciously or by default, a management decides whether or not to employ each device and in what form and to what degree.

Although a firm may concentrate on one particular sales promotion device, it almost invariably employs many of them to some degree. Even firms which rely primarily upon the appeal of low price must d some advertising; if they were not to do so, their low price offerings might not be noticed by many customers. Moreover, they are generally compelled to give some assurance of acceptable quality (by guarantees or return privileges). The point urged here is that each firm must employ a combination of sales promotion devices, rather than only one, and that the overriding task of marketing management consists in selecting the optimum combination. The formulation of a combination of sales promotion devices is sometimes described as the "Composition of a marketing mix" for an actual firm.

1. The selection of a marketing mix must be made very explicitly in terms of the particular market segments whose patronage is to be sought most intensively.
2. To a considerable degree, the individual sales promotion devices are substitutes for one another. One could spend more on advertising or to hire personal salesmen

of higher quality, or to build more quality into the product, etc.

3. Almost every one of the possible sales promotion devices must be employed in some form ad to some degree. No single line of appeal for patronage will suffice.

4. In deciding how much to rely upon each sales promotion device, the following general rules should be applied:

   (a) Never expend sums for sales promotion unless you anticipate that they will produce enough additional revenue to cover all of the costs incurred to obtain that revenue—including the sales promotion outlay. (One must take account of the effect of a sales promotion outlay on future sales as well as their immediate impact.)

   (b) Compare alternative sales promotion devices that might be employed to obtain any specified increase in sales volume and employ that one which involves least cost.

Connection Between "Scientific Marketing" and Market Strategy

Executives with responsibility in the marketing area will find maximum opportunity to apply the scientific method if they consciously endeavour to formulate a concrete market strategy. Preferably, this formulation will take a written form, and be quite explicit and detailed. A market strategy combines explicit ends and the means selected to achieve them; the scientific method can be employed to a considerable degree to assess the effectiveness of alternative measures for attaining any given objective.

Specifically, top marketing executives will be entitled to regard themselves as 'scientific' if they carry out the following steps:

1. Formulate each problem clearly and sharply, and in a form that lends itself to maximum verification by

the use of evidence.

2. Gather available evidence bearing on the problem.
3. Arrange for the collection of additional information that would contribute to a solution to the problem—within the financial means of the firm.
4. Organize and analyze the information gathered in a manner that will shed maximum light on the solution to the original problem.
5. Formulate conclusions suggested by the evidence into hypotheses, such of which implies a potential solution to the original problem.
6. Test the hypotheses to the fullest extent possible.
7. Make a list of alternative solutions to the problem that has been discarded in favour of the one selected.

Historical Antecedents of the Marketing Strategy Concept

When a new concept stands by itself, its meaning and significance often are unclear. It contrasted with other views and seen as part of a general progression of ideas, it generally can be understood and appraised rather easily. Accordingly, the notions which preceded the marketing strategy concept will be described very briefly. Historians recording the process of intellectual discovery invariably conclude that thought develops in an orderly, step-by-step method. Whether this view is valid or is the creation of the historian themselves sometimes is unclear. Consequently, the following sketch of the marketing strategy concept's development may not describe how individuals came by their idea; it does, however describe the state of thinking at successive points in time.

The marketing strategy concept attempts to organize the factors that determine the sales of individual products. We must therefore seek its antecedents among the writings of men who were interested in explaining or actually influencing the volume of sales. The earliest probably would be the merchants of ancient times and the early Green philosophers who occasionally wrote about commercial affairs. Given the modest purposes at hand, this review will pass over the early writings and will start with the "Classical" economists.

Although they doubtless knew that they were oversimplifying the matter, classical economists based their explanations of sales solely on the effect of price. (All other possible influences were held constant and left unexplored.) They offered a simple and monolithic view of the determination of sales that was later incorporated into the demand schedule. In their view, sales varied inversely with price—at any given time and with all other things remaining equal; later economists summarized the relationship between sales and price in the "law of Demand."

The second stage in the attempts of professional economists to explain the determinants of sales might be dated from the publication of Edward Chamberlin's "theory of Monopolistic Competition."[1] It was during this stage that academic economists first took explicit account of non price influences n sales. Professor Chamberlin explored the effects of advertising on sales and explained this factor in the traditional manner common to formal economics. Despite the fact that the "Theory of Monopolistic Competition" was written over a quarter of a century ago, many academic discussions of sales still proceed as if price were the overwhelmingly important determinant of sales. Little attention is devoted even now to non price influences on sales by economists, although several books have been written by academic economists on the subject of individual nonprice influences on sales.

At this stage, the development of concepts to explain product sales reached a fork in the road. One prong continued the application of traditional techniques to take account of a larger number of influences on sales. An important step in this direction was taken in 1941 when Professor Kenneth Boulding2 treated sales efforts and costs in the same way that theorists had handled production costs; this theoretical framework contained the implicit analogy between the to marketing executive and the engineer. Economists have not built on this major breakthrough, however. An article by P.J. Verdoorn in 19563 represents perhaps the high point of this line of development, which is characterized by the use of geometric tools of analysis.

Further developments along this traditional route are in the hands of persons with a mathematical orientation. The field of operations research known as "programming" handles many sales promotion activities without serious difficulty, because mathematics is vastly more powerful than geometry. Programming of sales activity is not being explored by formal economics but represents the contribution of marketing specialists in the main.

The second fork in the road reached after the writing of the "Theory of Monopolistic Competition" might be termed the checklist approach to the sales problem. It was along this road that the term "marketing mix" was introduced for the first time by Professor Neil Borden in approximately 1953.[4] Writers who have followed this route were concerned with two major factors: First, they sought to itemize the large number of influences upon sales that marketing executives must take into account; second, they were interested in facilitating practical application of the concept to concrete operating problems. Foremost among the writers who adopted this approach were Professors Neil Bordenand Albert Frey,[5] The latter attempted to relate the marketing mix concept directly to the development of marketing programmes in his publication, which carries the subtitle, "Programming for Optimum Results."

With the development of the checklist approach, the enormity of the problem confronting the top marketing executive became apparent. The task of balancing a very large umber of variables (even if one ignores their interdependence) clearly is huge. Paucity of evidence about the productivity of individual sales promotion devices, and the difference between present and future markets inevitably makes the task of the chief marketing executive overwhelming, if not impossible. The inability to see down a workable method of composing a marketing mix is not a failing of the concept itself; the concept does describe what the top marketing executive should attempt to do. It certainly represents a substantial improvement over earlier views that took explicit account of only a few factors influencing sales. The complexity of the sale function is real and not a figment of the imagination of the concept builders.

Doctrine discussing determinants of sales had reached this state when the concept of marketing strategy was first set down in 1957. This concept differs form earlier thought on the subject by relating customer targets directly to the marketing mix. (It may be regarded as another step done with road from the checklist approach to the sales problem). It emphasizes that an effective marketing mix requires top management to be explicit about the kinds of customers to whom the business is trying to sell because specific sales promotion devices that appeal to some customer will bore others and even repel some.

The addition of customer targets to the concept of the marketing mix partly overcomes the difficulties in implementing the concept caused by a lack of information. When a marketing specialist is explicit. About his target customers and informs himself thoroughly about their needs, desires, perceptions, habits, attitudes, assumptions, economic situation, etc. He can guess more confidently about the productivity of different sales promotion devices than if he thinks in terms of so unrealistic and abstraction as "the average customer."

5

Theory, Process and Practice of Business Management

Business activities include manufacturing, commercial, trade and other economic activities of both individuals and institutions, viz., economic, social and political. In economic view point business sis production and distribution of goods and services on a continuous basis with a view to make profits. As in the words of Keith Daivs and Robert L. Blomstrom, business refers to the development and processing of economic values in society. Society is a social system that involves people and for their organization in relationships consisting of some observable whole. Business is the sub-system of the social system. Political system is the another dimension of the society which influence largely the business system. Business is an economic activity existing in the society as an institution.

Meaning of Management

There are man definitions of management giving different connotations. Most of the persons having touch with the management discipline are convinced to say that it is an organized effort of people whose purpose is to achieve the objectives and goals of an organization. To understand clearly the nature and meaning of management it is essential to review the view and ideas expressed by academicians and practitioners. Some authors considered management as an activity. An activity that is applicable to any kid of organisation and situation where human beings are involved as a group for the purpose of achieving some common goal. W. Jack Duncan defines "Management consists of all organisational activities that involves goal formation and accomplishment, performance appraisal and the development of an operating philosophy that ensures the organisation's survivals within the social system". In this definition Duncan gave us the tasks of management as goal formation, goal accomplishment and evaluation and implementation through follow-up. Organisations are dynamic processes within which individuals interact for the accomplishment of personal and collective goals. In such organisations manager has to set the goals for the individual people to accomplish the ultimate objective of that organisation. Then manager can develop the ultimate objective of that organization. Then manger can develop the means of a accomplishing the goal and thereby objectively measure success. It is an objective scientific procedure. Decision implementation is the most important part of the management where solutions to the problems are implemented. Thus there is management in labour unions, in religious institutions, in education, in agriculture, in the hospital, in the library and at home. Anywhere we find people gathered together as a group we need a team effort and group must function as a cohesive group. To achieve this cohesiveness we must have management.

Mc. Farland defines management as a process by which managers create, direct, maintain and operate purposive organisations, through systematic coordinated cooperative human effort. The term "process" emphasizes the dynamic or on going nature of management as activity varying spans of time Change is the most basic feature of organisations. In managing organisations managers create changes, adapt organizations to changes and implement changes successfully. Newman, Summer and Warren considered that management as a social process. In their view "management" is a process because it comprises a series of actions that lead to the accomplishment of objectives. It is a social process because these actions are principally concerned with relations between people. George R. Terry defines management as "a distinct process which is aimed at accomplishing stated goals by the use of human resources and other resources."

Donnely, Gibson and Ivencerich also support the view of management as a process. But their stress is more on coordination. According to them, management is a process by which individual and group effort is coordinated toward group goals. In order to achieve goals through a group coordination is essential and management involves securing and maintaining this co-ordination. Henry Koontz and O'Dnnell strongly stressed the necessity of coordination effort for management. According to them. "Management is the creation and maintenance of an internal environment in an enterprise where individuals working together in groups, can perform efficiently and effectively towards the achievement of group goals."

Many writers have defined management as a function rather than a process. Luther Gulick defines that management includes planning, organizing, staffing, directing, coordinating reporting, and budgeting. He coined the word POSDCORB from the initial letters of management functions which has become quite popular in usage. Dunu, Stephens, and Kelley contend that management is a role which includes a set of duties, responsibilities, and relationships involved in work organisations these duties and responsibilities constitute the functions of a manager. Henry Fayol contend that" to manage is to forecast and plan, to coordinate" According to James Fundy "Management is principally a task of planning, coordinating, motivating and controijing the efforts of others towards a specified objective" These functions definitions help up to study the subject matter of management as the managerial job break down into its actual components.

Theo Haimann has used the term' management' to denote

the meanings of the activity, process and functional concepts. In one sense the term refers to one group or body of persons having an activity to accomplish. In another sense management as a process includes planning, organization, directing' controlling and coordinating. And finally management as a discipline refers to a body or knowledge ad practice comprising of above stated functions.

Over fifty-five years ago Mary Parker Follette defined management as "getting things through people" It looks very simple. According to this definition managers do not do things; they get other people to do things. Harold Koontz modified this definition by saying that "arrangement is the art of getting this done through and with people in the formally organized groups. It is the art of creating an environment in which people can perform as individuals and yet cooperate towards the attainment at group goals. It is the art of removing blocks to such performance, a way of optimizing efficiency in reaching goals". Though the definitions of this kind stress on supervising and the human resources of the organisation, they mislead us it hut focusing fully on the managerial role. Managers spend a very high proportion of their time not only with their subordinates, but also with their superiors and their equals and as well as with a great range of individuals outside the firm.

The mission of the business is to develop and process the economic values of the society. In doing so business should consist of some infrastructure to function. The Infrastructural requirements of the business are internal and external. The internal requirement includes, premises, raw-material, machines, power, finance, technique, methods and personnel. The role of personnel is unique as it is the most and personnel. The role of personnel is unique as it is the most inevitable factor to accomplish things. Without people machines cannot be operated, raw material will note supplied with product, funds may not be arranged in proper time. The success of the business also depends on the ability of business firm to deal with various outside people like, customers, suppliers, bankers, investors, government officials, union officials, competitors, trade association Officials, the press and politicians.

To understand and to work with such varied groups of people businessmen should know ho they act and react and Why they behave as they do. Since business involves the analysis of people in a variety of economic and social relationships, simply the study of business will be known as the study of people.

To achieve success the business should process the right type, quantity and quality of various inputs i.e. material, power, premises to convert the raw material into finished product, the method of production, money to finance all facet of the business activity, the markets which can readily absorb the products and the best talents of ma-power to get done all thee things manpower that is the last ingredient supersedes all other elements as nothing will happen unless somebody does something. The success of business lies with the ability to manage people. Altogether managing the people in the right way I the necessary ingredient to achieve success in business. Because people with various business abilities viz., effective decision making, decision, implementation, cooperating with others, communication, planning and organising the things, are required to handle business activities. The above analysis gives us the idea that management is inevitable and it is an important function to be practiced in business to achieve success.

Definition:

No single definition discussed in the above paragrahs touches the entirely of the essence of management. But a very comprehensive definition was given by a team of academicians of the United States business schools in around 1940. The team aimed at deciding a definition that businessmen would accept and practice and that academician would teach. According to that team:

"Management is guiding human and physical resources

into dynamic organisation units that attain their objective to the satisfaction of those served and with a high degree of morale an sense attainment on part of those rendering the service."

According to this definition management consists the following five ingredients.

Management involves guiding human and physical Resources: A manager must balance between these two resources. He can not put more emphasis on physical resources and ignore human resources or vice-versa. He should not neglect people over technology. There should be equal concern for human and as well as physical resources.

Dynamic Nature of the Orgnisation: The environment in which rganisations are existing is dynamic. The environment is subject to change which brings stresses on organisations. For example changes in technology, market conditions, competitive products and services, attitudes of customers demands the organization to adapt timely measures to achieve the predetermined goal. Managers must be competent to prediction advance of these changes so as to make able the organisation to readily adapt to such changes in the environment. Such organisations are said to be dynamic. Thus management make organisation to become dynamic.

Attainment of Objective: Attainment of predetermined objective will be the ultimate goals of the organization which should be accomplished by the management. The purpose of the organisation should not be lost. Goal realisation is the mission of the management. Goals may differ from organisation to organization but the task of management is to reach such goals.

Measurement of Performance: The performance in regard to attainment of objectives can be measured through the degree of satisfaction derived by those who are served. The public or the consumers are the people who are served by the organisations. Hence the consumer satisfaction should be the prime concern of the management. Management can become successful only through attaining consumer satisfaction.

High Degree of Morale of those who Render Service: This segment of the definition refers to members of employees of an organisation. It is the management's responsibility to see that all the employees are happy with the organisation. The level of their morele, and sense of belongingness to organisation strongly influence the success of the organisation. Because the kid of satisfaction derived from their work will have impact on the achievement of their individual goals ultimately the organisational goal. Thus management tries to maintain high level f morale among the employees.

In brief management is attainment of the objective through harnessing the resources giving equal importance to human and physical resources where the satisfaction of the served and employees will be the prime concern.

Management – Organisation Administration

Management, Organisation, Administration are the three words most commonly used in the management literature. They attribute rather confusing meaning because of the failure to distinguish among fundamental concept. It is not even necessary to define those terms restricting their scope to the fields of activity tat they designate.

Organisation Vs Management: Refers to the mechanism or structure that enables people to work effectively. In view of George R. Terry "Organisation is the arrangement of functions deemed necessary for attainment of the objective and is an indication of the authority and the responsibility assigned to individuals charged with the execution of the respective functions. In a nut—shell organisation is a basic structure having established relationships between various factors. It is the task of designating the departments and the and power that are to carryon the work, defining their function and specifying relations that should exist between various departments and individuals. Organisation is in total a mechanism of management and where management is attainment of the objective through guiding human and physical resources at the utmost satisfaction of those served and those rendering service.

Administration is the function in the industry concerned in the determination of corporate policy the coordination of finance, production and distribution, the settlement of the compass of organisation and the ultimate control of executives". On the other hand management is the execution of policy within the limits set up by the administration for the particular objects et before it.

Breach regards management as an all inclusive function involving responsibility for the effective planning and regulation or guidance of operation of an enterprise. According to Breech: "Management is the total process of executive control and administration is that part of management which is connected with the installation and carrying out of the procedures by which the progress of the activities is regulated and checked against plans".

Fayol and Newman do not make any distinction between the two terms-administration and management. But when the two words are used to indicated different functions and not the persons who perform those functions. The distinction assumes much importance.

Taking all these views into account, and on the basis of the generally accepted view we may say that administration means overall determination of policies and major objectives. Whereas management is an executive function which is the active, direction human efforts. It is the work that a manager does as he seeks to get results through other people. It may be reiterated that administration as a function is largely determinative and management is essentially executive and organisation in the basic structure that is necessary to carryout these functions.

Management as a Profession

Science may be described as a systematic body of knowledge pertaining to an are events or phenomena. It maybe classified into two groups (I) Positive science and (ii) Normative Science, the first deals with what is and the other with what ought to be'.

Art refers to the way of doing a specific thing. It indicates how an objective is to be achieved. Art means the 'knowing how' the application. Whereas under science one normally understands the 'knowing why'.

If management is considered as an art, expertise in this field can only e gained by practice. Like any other art, mastering the profession of management requires practice. This practice gives an intuitive knowledge to solve various organizational and managerial problems. Only by experience and practice one gains such knowledge. If management is regarded as science, organisational and managerial problem-requires the knowledge and application of scientific methods and techniques.

Management fails to stand for the tests of either science or art, because management discipline contains both the characteristics of science and art. Te science of management provides a body of principles or law for guidance in the solution of specific management problems and objective evaluation of results. On the other hand, the art of management deals with application of skill and effort for producing desirable results on situation in specific cases.

Art and science of Management complement each other and thus, are not mutually excusive. With every increase in the knowledge of science, the art is b[illegible]d to be improved. Management art and management scie[illegible] are inter-woven and overlapping nature. Art of management is an old as human civilization but the science of 'management is an event of recent past.

Recently considerable attention has been given to analytical approaches to management resulting in the emergence of mathematical formulae business games, operational research and scientific decision-making.

Management science is not regarded as exact a science as physics or chemistry. Koontz O "Donnel and Weihrich commented that management as an inexact science. It is a social science and hence it is subject to certain limitations. The dynamic nature of business situations and the nature of human behaviour are subject o produce uncertainties and to that extent the science or management functions less exactly.

A profession has been defined as an occupation in which one professions to have acquired specialized knowledge which is used either in instructing, guiding or advising others. A full-fledged profession usually has the following characteristics:

1. An organised and systematic body of knowledge.
2. A formal method of acquiring knowledge and skill through established institutions.
3. Establishment of professional associations.
4. Growth or professional consults.
5. Professional code and conduct.
6. Licensing to restrict the entry of others not having the requisite qualifications.

Management profession has almost all the characteristics mentioned above except that it does not require licensing of mangers nor it does restrict the entry of people into this profession Who do not have specialized training. The systematic development or management associations and consultants prove that management is a developing profession. But it cannot be described as a full-fielded profession like medicine or low, unless there is a professional conduct and licensing of managers. Some academicians content, that the master of business administration degree should constitute the minimum pre-requisite forentering the profession of management. But petr Drucker the father of modernmanagement opposes thisidea by stating that "no greater harm couldbe opposes this idea b stating that "no greater harm coudlbe doneto economyor to society than to professionalise management thruhlicensing requirements or specifying special academic degrees as necessary training." Beside the educational qualification several other factors which influence his performance must be taken into consideration.

Universality of Management

Management functions are having the universal applicability. As stated earlier the functions of management viz. planning, organising, staffing, directing and controlling are practiced similarly in the organisation irrespective of their basic structure, goals, environment and nature of business. This is know as universality of management, it is clear from the fact that management continued its development as an increasingly sophisticated discipline. Today management is accepting the administration challenges of even not for-profit organisations in government, education, charitable, service and healthy-care environment.

In all forms of organisations either profit making or non-profit making the practice of functions of management is one and the same but the technique of performing these functions may differ from organisation to organisation having relation to its basic structure goals, environments and nature of business, Here a distinction should be made between function and technique. Function is the task that should be accomplished whereas technique is the way of performing that function. Management functions are quite similar in all organisations in the universe despite their diverse characteristics. Hence we can talk about the universality of management. The limitation is that organisation may select dissimilar techniques to perform these universally accepted functions. In all forms of enterprises and at all levels of organisations the environment of management can certainly differ. However, management itself is essentially the same process.

6

Functions of Business Management

Management is an activity which is undertaken on a continuous basis. So much of significance has been attached to it in this 20th century with the advent of the complexity of the modern organisations. As the organisations are rightly described as socio-technical systems, they need the people who can lead them towards the achievement of the goals. Peter F. Drucker rightly pointed out that the manager is the dynamic, life giving element in every business; and without his leadership the resources never become production. But management is the least known of our organisations. Simply management may be regarded as what a manager does. Thus management has become the specific organ of the business organisations as in the words of Peter. F. Drucker "The enterprise can decide, act and behave only as its managers do by itself the enterprise has no effective existence.

Managing is so complex that our minds cannot consider all its facts at the same moment, it is needed to dissect the managerial activity into parts in order to grasp the full significance of each part. Then the question arises what is the managerial activity? Theo Haiman puts it at the right way by saying that "we can recognize a manager by the functions he performs, and these are managerial in nature"

There is no exception to the fact that the manager might perform a non-managerial function to fill in or to help out. And it is clear that a non-manager does not perform a managerial function. Coming to the functions performed by a manager various authors classified in different manner.

Henry Fayol described the managerial functions as planning, organising, commanding, co-ordinating and constituting. In this classification, the term commanding is much autocratic in nature. Co-ordinating need not be considered as a separate function of Management because co-ordination is the essence of management Luther Gultick divided the managerial activity into planning, organising, staffing, directing, co-ordinating, reporting and budgeting (PoSDCORB). Gultick used the term 'representation' which appear to classify the activity of the managers who represent their organization in maintenance of external relations. To create better image for the organisation in the a society not only managers representing it responsible but also all other employees, whether managerial or not. In other words there is no necessity to consider that representation as depatate function. When it is the responsibility of all people in the organization. Coming to the budgeting, in the modern time is used as a tool of planning, rater than as a separate function of management.

According to Peter F. Drucker, the task of managing is:

(a) managing the business sin a positive manner, i.e., by taking actions which make the desired results come to pass.

(b) Managing the managers which refers to setting the goasfor the management people in the organisation. It is a task of creating productive enterprise out of human enterprise.

(c) Managing workers and work which means, organising work to make it suitable for worker and also organising people to make them work productively and effectively.

In the most common usage, many well know authors like Theo Haimann, Koontz O Donnell etc, classified managerial functions as planning, organizing, staffing, directing, and controlling. There the question arises about the order in which the managerial functions should be undertaken Koontz, O'Donell states that "planning comes first, organising staffing, leading (Directing) and controlling enterprise carriers out only one master plan, each part o which, once completed, never has to be revised or modified. This conception is unrealistic. In practice, managers oversee many plans in various stage of execution and may involve in solving a control problem. Thus managing is a systematic network of activities which does not necessarily follow a sequential order. However, for the sake of clarity and simplicity in the following paragraphs management functions will be discussed in a sequential order.

Planning

Planning is deciding in advance what should be done in the future to achieve the stated goal of he organisation. It consists of selecting the organisational objectives, programmes, policies, procedures and strategies either for the entire enterprise of for any part of it, The meaning or planning fells us that is the most basic of all management functions as it involves in the decision making process.

As plans are means to achieve some ends with the exception of a few routine activities, every organisational managerial activity requires planning. Planning is a must in bringing out and promoting the new products in distributing, pricing the products, selecting the people and assigning them with the roles, in acquiring the finances, credit and so on.

Nature of Planning

The nature of the planning can be stated as follows:

1. Planning is the primary function of management. All other functions flow from planning.
2. Planning is pervasive. Managers at every point and

at every level of organisation have the element of planning in their working. It is not the function of the top boss only or alone.

3. Planning has analytical as well as initiative aspects. The first is based on facts or information and the second is related to experience.

4. Planning involves decision and action, and both are related with timing. Planning must lead to decisions, and decision must result in actions, otherwise planning becomes meaningless.

5. Planning is a preparation of a plan of action. It is a mixed part of every managerial action of function. It is not a separate, recognizable act.

6. Planning is essentially a mental exercise in thinking. We may not know that there is a Gresham's law in planning. Just as bad money tends to drive good money out of circulation easy routine drives out hard planning work.

7. Planning is a continuous activity of an executive, It is a continuing task because group activity goes on always.

8. Planning is done in advance of work. All the related details and relationships are worked out before the activity starts.

9. Planning requires decision-making in selecting a desired course or action.

10. Some people believe that planning starts after the objective of the enterprise is set. Others thin that objective setting is the first task of planning function.

Planning is the duty of a responsible manager in the organization, Planning function cannot be delegated to non-manager. But such non-managers can assist in preparation of plans.

Organising

The organising function includes the dividing and assigning the roles to the people with enough authority and responsibility to achieve the enterprise objectives and goals. It means granting of all the activities in the enterprise, dividing them among the departments and assigning these activities to the groups of people. In order to accomplish this task managers establish an intentional structure of roles through determination of the activities required to achieve the goals of an enterprise. In doing so, managers delegate necessary authority to their subordinates to carry the activities assigned. In the organisation function the primary of co-ordination can be recogniased. Because, the responsible manager has to co-ordinate the activities of his subordinates. It means the organising functions aimed at establishment and maintenance or informational relationships, horizontally and vertically in the enterprise. It is thus, creation of structural relationship by which an enterprise is bound together and the frame work in which individual effort is co-ordinated.

The creation of this structural relationships expresses itself in the form of an organisation structure. All the functions of management are carried out within this organisation structure. Organisation structure is invisible framework which, formally for informally establishes the authority, responsibility status and roles of each person in relation to all other persons in the group through specified communication channels. The organisation structure is not an end in itself but a tool for accomplishing enterprise objectives. The application of an efficient organising function is important as it contributes towards, the goal achievement. But striving much for organisation structure without its applicability, efficiency and use is futile. The organisational structure must reflect the goals that are targeted to achieve by the enterprise and as well as the environment .

There are several types of organisation in existence, formal and informal profit and non-profit, service and manufacturing: public and private etc. An analysis of the nature of organisng function help us to understand clearly its importance. In the following lines the characteristics of organizing function has been explained.

1. Organization sympolises a group effort.
2. Organizing rises when the business sis first established and when basic policy hanges necessiate change.
3. Organizing establishes interrelationships among the people in the organisation and creates a formal structure of personal inter relationships.
4. Through this function the role of an individual and his position in the organisation will be specified. And this task is done by determining the acceptable and expected forms of behaviour of the people.
5. Organizing activity will become fruitful by co-ordination. Coordination is essential to achieve the group effort. With the help of coordination human actions that are harmful to the enterprise will also be regulated.
6. Organizing provides the necessary scope to integrate the enterprise internally and externally.
7. Organisational policies and frame work, provides the enterprise with the necessary flexibility to change its mission and the direction of activity as an when it is required.
8. Organizing is the way to promise continuity permanence to the enterprise.

Organization is therefore the creation of a structure relationship by which an enterprise is bound together and the framework in which individual effort is co-ordinated aimed at achieving the ultimate goal.

Staffing

Simply manning the organisational structure is known as staffing. The Haimann stated that "staffing involves selection and training of future, managers". More particularly, staffing is known as keeping the jobs in the enterprise filled with the right people. Hence staffing function attempts to fin the right person for each job. Selecting finding a right person is not all what the staffing function refers to. After finding a person appropriate training should be imparted to him. Then such person should be inducted to the right job. The selected candidate should be compensated with the proper remuneration and benefits. Above all these staffing function also includes periodical appraisal of the performance of the people carrying out the jobs. These are the various facts of the staffing function.

Staffing, therefore, is the most crucial job of management, as enterprise's task should only be achieved through the people selected. A mistake that is committed in staffing function will ultimately affect adversely each and every organ of the organization. Hence one can imagine its strategic position in the managerial functions. Managers discharge in the staffing function requires to be more vigilant as the manpower requirements of the enterprise change very often. The staffing function cannot be done once for all, since many changes take place in the organisations due to retirement and death creation of new positions, turnover etc.

Directing

In carrying out the day-to-day work, by the people in the organisations several problems may arise which seeks proper direction to overcome them. To avoid this situation in the organisation managers are charged with the task of directing. Directing includes guiding, teaching, coaching, supervision, and issuing directive for the accomplishment of subordinates. Directing, therefore, is the manager's job to develop the abilities of the subordinates to carryout the organizational plans and also to induce and activate the people to use their abilities for the achievement of common goal. Directing in nutshell is shaping the favourable behaviour of the people through careful guiding and attainment of the goals.

In directing manager strive to integrate the needs of people with the welfare of his enterprise. He has to recognize the desires of the people and at the same time he had to identify necessity or cooperation and efficiency required for the success of the enterprise. It means a leader tries to achieve the organisational success through employee motivation. Achievement of such balance between individual motivation and organisational success is not always easy. But establishing two way communication, assisting subordinates to perform their duties, and helping them to achieve their personal aspirations or activities that induce voluntary cooperation. This kind of behaviour by a leader also fosters an atmosphere of trust, respect and confidence between himself and his sub-ordinate.

The above discussion states about the steps that are involved in the directing functions, they are:

1. Establishment of inter-relationships among the people in the organisation linking the master plan of the company and immediate activity to be carried out.
2. Specifying the nature and type of the jobs to be performed by the people.
3. Pointing out the specific individuals to carry out the work.
4. Establishment of communication channels with the individuals and informing them about the assignments.
5. Providing a vigilant and concurrent supervision from time to time direct the people towards the achievement of goal.
6. Motivating the people in the right perspective and also helping them to possess high morale.
7. Taking effective steps to maintain discipline in the organisation.

In organisations, clear direction coupled with a spirit

of cooperation, typically achieves the necessary coordinated effort. And some occasions may be happened to a leader to become tough, hold people to high standards of performance, discipline wisely and occasionally make use of power.

Tough, hold people to high standards of performance, discipline wisely and occasionally make use of power.

Controlling

Controlling is a function of management which provides the knowledge about the conformity of plans. Manger's job will not be finished until ad unless he determines how well the jobs have been done and what progress is being made towards the goal. It consists the job of determining what is actually happening, evaluating the performance and what changes are needed to make if the organisation is deviating from the plans.

The concept of control envisages the following items:

1. It provides a historical record of the things happened in the enterprise.
2. It measures the performance of people against goals and plans.
3. It shows clearly the positive and negative deviations that exists.
4. It explains with reasons why such negative deviations were happened.
5. It provides the effective solutions to take corrective actions.
6. It enables the managers to identify trends in costs markets in all aspects of business.
7. It provides guide for future action.
8. To exercise this function several devices like budgets inspection records, accounting, reports, managerial reports ad control charts will be used.

There is a misunderstanding about the person who exercise the control function. Some people contend that top managers in the organisation generally undertake the job of controlling. This sort of attitude is prevalent mainly due to the fact that they view control supervision, and discipline in the same way. They consider control as the tight supervision and discipline only be maintained by the superiors. But as Koontz and O'Donnell states "Control is the function where by every manager from president to foreman should make sure that what is done, and what is intended.

To speak strictly controlling and planning are interwoven and more specifically planning must precede controlling. Plans are not self achieving and there is not meaning of controlling unless objectives are specified and policies and rules to be followed properly determine.

Importance of the Functions:

The various functions of management enumerated above are all part of the manager' so, the importance attached to each one may vary at different times and in different planes.

1. In times of income decline a company is naturally disposed to scrutinize expenditure more carefully and on the other hand attention may shift to planning for expansion.

2. Problems as a result of widespread expansion may be reconciled with new ways of coordinating internal and external activities.

3. Within the framework of above functions of managers shall be able to concentrate upon innovations. It is a heartfelt fact to note many firms are owning and maintaining special Research and Development swings.

4. To expose the image of the organisation. The functional managers can take necessary steps by reporting to the society by making clear what has deen done by their units in reducing, air and water pollution,

providing employment and last but not least to the national exchequer.

5. The over size of the business units require the most professional management which carryout all the functions stated above with a mission and zeal to reach the goal.

All the managers right from the chief executive to the supervisor in the shop floor shall be participating in performing these functions. But the intensity of participation differ from position to position of the managers.

7

Theory and Principles of Business Management

Management as a coordinating body helps the enterprise to organize the entire activities in such a manner as to enable it to attain the predetermined objectives. Management is accepting the challenges of organising and coordinating the tasks of diversified organisations. It necessities the development of principles of management which may be regarded as the basic truths to check the applicability of managerial actions. And so important the theory of management which guide the managerial team on right lines throughout its endeavour in achieving the goals. Principles and theory thus, provides a structural framework to the organisation to activate upon.

To ensure greater precision and to avoid personal judgement there is every need of theory and principles of management. As management is the discipline having universal applicability, the controversy may arise in accepting its generalization. In such circumstances developed set of principles and theories may help a lot to subdue the controversy.

The development of a conceptual frame work of the theory of management helps the teaching and training of the managers. In the absence of developed theory and principles is quite difficult to undertake the job of teaching management.

This discussion leads us to a doubt about the meaning

of theory and principles of management the task to be performed by them and their relevance in the present conditions of business. In the following paragraphs an attempt is made to find out answers to the questions.

Principles of Management

Terry defines that "principle is a fundamental statement or truth providing a guide to thought or action". The fundamental statement applies to a series of phenomena under consideration and signifies what results to expect when the principles if applied. I principle thus is rule of conduct which must be followed in a particular activity. Keontz O' Donnell and Weihrich consider that "the most meaningful principles are those which involves casual relationships with dependent and independent variables'. They further referred as descriptive prescriptive of r normative. A principle is descriptive if it merely describes a relationships between variables. A principle is prescriptive or normative, if it is stated in such a way to indicate what a person should do. They further argue when principles are applied against some scale of values, they may be referred to as prescribing action or as being prescriptive or normative. It is the goal of all managers to operate in such a way as to accomplish he goals of organisation, by applying management principles against the values possessed by them. It means with the help of principles of management managers can avoid fundamental mistakes in their work and may be confidently in a position to foretell results of their efforts." Principles of management set a normative path that a person should follow in attaining the goals of the organisation. They indicate destination point to the managers. Principles simplifies the process of management. Without principles the work of the manager will become a process in disorder and the result of the activities will become futile.

Thee are basic principles of management that are reasonably well established accepted and used. These principles of management represent the latest developments in the discipline. As the reliable knowledge is gained about it new principles will emerge and the same time, other management principles will be modified and some discarded, as not being truly representative of management knowledge.

Nature of Principles

Terry has sumarised the characteristics of principles of management in the following manner.

1. Principles are basic and they are not absolute.
2. They are neither laws, nor dogmas,
3. Principles are working hypothesis.
4. Principles only describe and predict. They do not state what sought to be until the uses employed them with particular set of values.
5. The applicability of management principles depends, on individuals, knowledge and the ability to judge.
6. Principles have some flexibility in their application taking into account the particular, special or changing conditions.

This principles of management are the guiding facts to the managers in making fruitful their endeavour.

Essentials of Principles

In describing the essentials of principles of management Terry has stated that principles should be:

(a) Practical which means they can be put to use in any circumstance.

(b) Relevant to a broad spectrum of business situations

(c) Consistent in giving similar results in identical situations.

Role Played by Management Principles

The principles of management as the fundamental truths

and their interrelationships in the area of management, do score of favours to a business executive. For the sake of clarity of understanding, they can be marshaled in the following categories.

(i) Efficiency of an executive is increased: the principle of management improves efficiency of executives to a considerable extent. These principles broke out of experiences and they can be applied in a situation. It saves the executive from training basic research that may leave little time and energy for him undertake other important tasks. These principles are like "readymade solution" or "instant guide lines" applicable in a particular situation.

    Events are likely to recur in future with a insignificant amount of change in their basic character. The five honour principles of management can be applied to these situations with appropriate modifications depending upon the special circumstances. This vastly boosts up the efficiency of an executive, who can produce better results now.

(ii) Management principles give a definite and concrete shape to Management. Principles of Management provide a comprehensive framework within which all problems of management can be included. A clear conceptual understanding of the principles comes in handy in solving and analysing problems. In case of no principles the managers shall solve them in an unscientific manner. Either the problems will be in adequately solved, or in a few cases, certain problems shall await the development of adequate science and systematized knowledge, it there is not set of already known and practiced principles. The training of the manager is facilitated happily enough to a good extent, with the teaching of principles of management.

(iii) To conduct research, management principles provide a good mental food: The science of management is still in its evolutionary process. It is but natural for the academicians as well as practitioners to conduct research in the area of management (i) to correctly verify the relevance of old principles in the modern context and (ii) to revalidate the relevance of the principles in their original context. This process for searching the truth not only pertaining to past but also present enhances the exiting knowledge. New and better methods of management are discovered. The management science is vastly benefited.

(iv) Management principles increase human welfare also. The principles of management guide the executive in harnessing the resources, which are scarce and invaluable in the best possible manner. They indicate that these resources should be used in a manner as to yield the highest possible returns. This increases the wealth of enterprise itself and that of society at large.

The efficiency is increased by availability of instant solutions. This may be used in projects providing a high amount of profits. This will be distributed among the elements of society and thus increasing the welfare to the people living in society. In any social system the aim is to maximize the welfare to the people living in society. In any social system the aim is to maximize the welfare of its constituents and principles of management make the task simple, distinct and essay.

Theory of Management

Theory is a systematic grouping of inter-related principles. Koontz and his associates further state that its task is to tie together significant knowledge to give it a frame work. Theo Haimann contends that theory is a body of principles dealing with the subject matter systematically. On the other hand Arnold Russel defines "theory is an integrated body of definitions, assumptions and general prepositions conveying a subject matter from which a comprehensive behavior and a consistent, specific oftenable principles can be deducted logically.

According to this definition the theory of management is a set of interrelated principles, unifying and guiding managerial activities that are targeted to reach the ultimate goals in the real field of operations manager should possess the knowledge of the theory of management to observe, identify and explain the inter relationships among the people in the organisation. With that knowledge the manager can integrate together the activities of the people by understanding them fully. Managers job will be simplified and his effectiveness and efficiency increased. If the understands and properly interpret theory of management.

It is comprehended that the nature of theory may be attributed as-

1. A matured state of science is a systematic theory.
2. It uses the general concepts in the field.
3. It integrates logically the different elements.
4. It encourages and becomes base for doing empirical research.
5. It requires clarity of concepts, namely, mental images of a thing formed by generalisation form particulars.

Henry Fayol, Chester I. Barnard and Alwyn Brown, the practical scholars of management, recognized many years ago the need for theory of management.

Role of Theory of Management

The knowledge of the principles, techniques and theory of management influence greatly the practice. Because there I a close correlation between theory and practice. Because there is a close correlation between theory and practice. Theory of management play significant role in the management of organisation, Due to its significance and inevitability there is a great need of theory of management.

Increases the efficiency of managers: When the theory of management is developed, proved, and used, the managerial efficiency will be increased, managers can become more, effective by implementing and observing the guidelines provided by the management theory.

Offers a Conceptual Scheme to Managers: Koontz, O' Donnel and Weihrich contend that concepts are the building blocks of theory and principles. Theory of management which is based on such clearly defined concepts shall certainly provide the managers with an absolutely specified scheme to follow. Inter-relationships within the organisations are clearly described for the understanding of managers. Their understanding capacity shall be improved and as a result it will not happen them to arrive at a definite conclusion basing on irrelevant facts gathered by him. Thus theory, guides managers in decision making.

Develops Executives: As theory of management is a set of facts that are empirically tested and found correcting situations the intellectual abilities of manager is greatly developed. It orients the manager to search for solutions in times of crisis.

Managers can apply this knowledge to the solution of new problems. Problem situations are not alike in all respects. Manager cannot simply draw the examples from his experience. A knowledge of theory of management shall help him applying the techniques and ways to sole the problems in purview of the past experience.

Management theory can solve the future problems. Management theory can be applicable to any situation in the ever changing business environment. Hence any sort of future problems artising in the ever changing environment may be solved.

The practice of trail and error can be replaced. As management theory provides the established guidelines to solve the problems that the trail and error method can be replaced. Instead of spending his energy and initiative making futile changes he can straight away find a solution.

It crystalises the nature of management: it is difficult to analyse the managerial job and to train managers, if the concepts, principles and techniques of managements are not clearly fined. The developed theory of management shall be based on the clear cut concepts and principles. It serves as a good base for training managers and analyzing their jobs.

It Improves research: the concepts and hypothesis developed in theories of management can be used to do research. Such researches can help to build further new theories. In total the horizon of management knowledge will be expanded.

It helps to achieve social goals: development of management knowledge shall help the people to attain social goals as it increases efficiency in use of human and material resources. Manager coordinates the efforts of people so that their social goals are realized. Theory of management further help the people to manage things well.

But it has been said that the works in theory does not always succeed in practice. Theo Haimann argues that if principles are fundamental truths, theory must be practicable and applicable, there is then no difference between theory and practice. But to state theory may not be exactly fit to a given situation and it is clearly known that the theory may be practicable or impracticable basing upon the nature of a situation.

Controvercy over the Relevance of the principles: Many people raised doubts over the validity or relevance of the principles of management. They regarded the principles of management as the platitudes. They argue that management principles are as old as human race and there is nothing newness in them.

But management principles and theory are fundamental truths. One cannot discard a thing by saying tat it is something which is truly known as therefore, there is not relevance it.

Any truth which is familiar does not cease to be a truth only on account of familiarity. It only snows the relevance and validity of the principles. But unfortunately there are some tendencies which led to the notion that management principles and theories are irrelevant. They are:

1. This misconception arises mainly due to inability and unwillingness of the people to understand the views of theories.

2. The tendency of executives to prove the wrong things as right and misapplication of principles lead to the idea that principles of management are not true.

3. The entire framework of principles of management may be disregarded simply reference to one principle which is not practically implemented.

4. Lack of fulfledged research in the area of business management is also contributed for the idea that management principles are not practicable.

In recent times this attitude got a change with the advent of the II World War many controls were imposed by the countries and the continuing influence of great depression compelled the managers to define their roles and devising principles of management. The growing size of the business needs growing markets and as well as the improved executives talents. All together competition in the business also increases the various factors necessitate the development of modern managerial techniques.

8

Role and Importance of Business Management

The role of management in the economic and social fields of the modern society cannot be overemphasized. With the advent of the 'division of labour' no individual can look-after his requirements-food, shelter and clothing. If men together in various enterprises, pooling the resources and exchanging their outputs with many other people or enterprises, they grasp the means to flourish. Here lies the role of management to make successful such group efforts. Indeed' management has to play its role in converting the disorganized resources of men, machine, material and money into want satisfying objects.

The needs of society are fast changing. Newman, Summer and Warrant listed some national priorities. They contend that management must deal with the following new demands.

1. Individual self-expression. The rising generation wants meaningful jobs-as the fruits of high productivity.
2. Race and Urban problems. Society must make racial equally meaningful inter woven with this is urban renewal.
3. Pollution control. Our material achievements are fast overtaking the finite capacity our natural

environment. As is painfully evident in the rises of air and water pollution.

4. Health, education and welfare. An over-increasing share of our natural resources is being directed into such things as medical care, education, public recreation, pensions.

5. Guns and butter: Our combined space and military expenditures are already on a scale chat challenges our ability to have both guns and butter.

Thus, management has become the most important organ of society specially charged with making resources productive.

Management, has to coordinate the activities of the business organisation, the society and other parties concerned. Business unit tries to reconcile their activities with the expectations of the society through management. Management is concerned with integrating the enterprise—externality and internally. External integration can be brought by the Management by establishing coordinal relations with the consumers, suppliers, public, Government and by having understand and implement the changes in the technological, ecological, legal, social and cultural factors. To integrate enterprise into system the management has to recognize the structural importance or various departments and to coordinate their activities to reach the ultimate goal of the organisation.

Management is the most dynamic discipline which generates life and momentum to the organisations. If helps them to become competent in the competitive situations. The ultimate goal of the enterprise can be reached effectively in time when management play its right role. Managements helps organisations to reach the maximum scale of operations. Ultimately the success and survival of the organization depends upon how efficiently the management plays its role.

Underdeveloped countries are having many challenges to meet right from providing their population with basic amenities to other important requirements of life. Management's responsibility in thee countries is to channelise and convert the productive resources into consumable goods and services. Unfortunately these productive resources are scarce in availability otherwise if available these countries are unable to use them productively. Managerial activity in these countries is being concerned with finding, securing, the available resources and utilizing them with greater efficiency. In case of scare resources. It is the responsibility of the management to find and develop alternative solutions.

It has been stated that management is people. As a significant segment of the society. Management is mainly concerned with the development of people. Management take a lot towards the making of citizens of a country. As human aims and belief are mostly realized through the establishment of diverse associations in our society management is called in all such organisations.

Importance of Management

Peter F. Drucker once commented that management in fact becoming central resource of developed nations and the basic need of the developing ones, as it contributed greatly to the economic development of advanced nations and has displayed on ability to contribute to the development of nations which are not so economically advanced. In all these countries management assumes an important responsibility to clear about and appreciate the complexity of life.

The importance of the study of management can be traced out from the following factors.

Effective Utilisation of Productive Resources:

Management takes the charge of transforming the productive resources into the form needs by man. Management undertakes the responsibility of mobilising the key factors of production. Management has to coordinate the activities that are generally undertaken within the organisations and takes the charge of establishing good relations with the outside world. Effective utilization of the productive resources can be accomplished by the management by influencing and motivating the people who are connected with the task towards the common goal.

Meet Social Needs

Management is an important element of the society, it has to look after the needs of the society. Society is a complex of people with diverse and dissimilar perceptions and goals in such a situation management in the right perspective can take the challenging role of satisfying all such demands of society. It is only because management problem arises where men join together. Society is a gigantic get together of human beings, hence the need of management.

Create Good Business Ecology

Business ecology is identified as the existence of business unit and its surrounding environment. Management handling efficiently the inter-relationship between organization and its environment. It creates good business ecology. Management by integrating the organisation with a complex of external forces like technology, science, culture and legal forces, it establishes good relations. Within the organisation, it coordinates the activities of all departments. As management can establish better relations with the internal and external environment, it is said in total good business ecology can be created. In such circumstances management can eliminate or at least can better manage the competition. In reference to the size of the business organisation modern management enables the enterpreneurs to prefer bigger and even the biggest size of organisation. The bigger size of the business creates many problems in relation to the large scale production, huge capital and large number of personnel. Management with the application of scientific methods and techniques can solve these problems.

Develops People

Management develops the people as goods citizens and also it can develop a pool of managers for tomorrow through its sophisticated methods of training and development. In other words a culture of management talent will be created on the line of availability to organizations.

The importance of management to an organisation is of such a range to expect, it performs the day to day tasks that are required to fulfill to reach the targeted efficiency.

9

Social Responsibilities of Business Management

Probably, no question has received more attention by business, government politicians and people in general in the past few years than the question of hat the social responsibility of business is. The same question originally aimed at business is now being addressed with increasing frequency to Government agencies and their leaders; universities non-profit foundations, charitable trusts an even churches. An awakened society is asking the managers of all kinds of organisations, what they are doing to discharge their social responsibilities, and why they are not doing more" It can not be overlooked as various kinds of organized enterprises have different missions that have been entrusted to them by this society. The mission of business sis the production and distribution of goods and services. The mission of a Police department is protection of the safety and welfare of the people. The mission of a highway department is the designing ad construction of designed high ways. The mission of university is teaching and research.

We should not hold business managers responsible for solving all manner of social problems. Another question arises, do private enterprises have improvement of the human environment as one of their basic directives? Those who answer "Yes", hold social responsibilities among their values.

Those answering "No', are opposed to social responsibilities the Pragmatic manager says.

At present all three of these of these values are held by managers. Historically' however, one of these values has been typical of most managers in a given period. Before 1100 A.D. business people tended to hold social responsibility as "trusteeship values. From 1100 to above 1800, they shifted towards pragmatic attitude. Adam Smith' Wealth of Nations' ushered in the entire social responsibility period (from about 1800 to 1930) since there has been a move back toward pragmatic or pre-social responsibility values. But in most periods all these values have existed together. Thus, Robert Owen, Oliver Sheldon and others in the 1800's were clearly in favour of social responsibility in an era when most business people were opposed.

Joseph Moquiry argues persuasively that social responsibility will become an objective of business and enter the decision making process by managers and entrepreneurs when (1) Social responsibility becomes an important value of managers and entrepreneurs and (2) When environmental process pressure the manager to accept these premises.

An analysis of the above shows that there are two graps 'anti' and 'pro' for social responsibility. The anti position has been called the profit ethic and the 'pro-position' the social ethnic. The 'profit ethic' deals with the primary objective of business sis to maximize profits and serve the interests of its owners. They held the view that 'the business of a business is business. If the enterprise pays out some of it profits and socially acceptable ends (Tax or profit) only the Government should tax. However, individual manager should be socially responsible, but in their own way. The followers of Adam Smit agree that when each business maximizes the profit, this owners the cost of everything and improve the economic well being of all.

In social ethic, the position holds that a business is responsible for many groups, besides owners – including employees and customers. Therefore profit maximization is not the only objective of a business. Some profit should be diverted to social responsibility projects in short run, which will lead to greater ability to survive and satisfactorily long run profits.

Some Definitions:

The term social responsibility of business man will be used frequently. It refers to the objectives of business men to pursue those policies, to make those decisions or to follow those lines of action which are desirable in terms of the objectives and values of society Synonyms for social responsibility are "public Responsibility", "Social Obligation" and "Business Morality."

There term doctrine of social responsibility will refer to he idea as voluntary assumption of social responsibility while business men are one might be a practicable means toward ameliorate economic problems and attaining more fully the economic goals we see. It can also be defined as the obligation which a business house owes to society. By social responsibility is meant the obligation firm to consider the impact of both its decisions and action in entire social system.

The social responsibility of business men a meaning only in relation to the goals or values which one see from our economic system. The doctrine of social responsibility rests up on the idea that business should be conducted with concern b the effects of business operations upon the attainment of valued social goals. Some of the goals which many thoughtful people would keep at least in principles, in terms of which social responsibilities of business must be defined.

1. High Standard of Living: This means an abundant, of goods and services available for consumption by the masses of the people and the substantial amounts of leisure, which such abundant makes possible. The position of high standard of living requires a high rate of production. Therefore this goal I often referred "High productivity" of 'abundance' goals.

2. Economic Progress: this means planning a high value up on technological progress leading to new methods of production and to new products. It is desirable to increase the plant and equipment, non-material capital in the form of education, training and energy of the workers. It is important to utilize he natural resources product so that progress will not be slowed down by lack of land and natural materials.

3. Economic Stability: Largely, as result of alternating inflation and wide spread unemployment great importance to economic stability as a goal is attached. To expect perfect stability in anything so dynamic as the economic system would be unreasonable. To expect perfect stability in anything so dynamic as the economic system would be unreasonable. But, it is imperfect to tamper fluctuations in economic activity.

4. Personal Security: the concern about insecurity due to unemployment, sickness, accident damage and death ha increased with the growth of these problems during the great depressions. Personal Security was considered important and that each person is responsible to provide for his contingents as a matter of collective responsibility. What was regarded as exclusively an individual family problem has become largely a social problem.

5. Order as a social goal is usually associated with the political system, it also has economic connotations. The attainment of order in economic life requires the regular flow of foods to the market, the systematic equalization of demand and supply in all markets and the absence of violent strife in economic relationships.

6. Justice: The concept of justice in economic affairs pertains to 'equality' in the distribution of income and brought defusion of opportunity for personal development and economic advancement. It includes

provision of wide access to education, improvement of neighbourhood and family environment, provision of public health services, sanctions against nepotism, and removal of restrictions based upon colour, race, national origin, religion, sex, etc, political opinion, physical appearance or social status.

7. Freedom: in he economic sphere freedom has man facets, just as it has in the political sphere. Moreover, for we very freedom this corresponding responsibility. The 'freedom of enterprise' refers to the right of an individual or group of individuals who organize such land, labour and capital as he owns one can command in the market to make the use of these resources in the production and distribution of goods and services. Another freedom is freedom of consumer choice having the right for any individual to buy whatever is for sale when he pleases with any purchasing power at his command. The third freedom 'the freedom of those of occupation' implies the right of each individual to decide the type of vocation to forward and to change his vocation are place of employment whenever he chooses The last one 'the freedom of organisation" refers to the right of individual to band together for common purposes.

8. Development of individual person: most human beings spent a large portion of their working hours in some form of economic activity. They functioned as workers, managers, buyers and sellers, consumers and as inventors Moreover, a large part of human relationship occurs in the work shop, gross, or, market place. This means the quality of human life is determined in large measure by the physical environment in which economic activity takes place. As professor clark has said "the individual is so molded body, mind, and character by his economic activities and relations. Stimul and disabilities, freedom and servitudes, that industry can truly be said to make the men and

women who work in it, noless truly that the commodities it turns out for the market'.

9. Community Improvement: Economic activity has a direct influence on the quality of the local community in which it occurs. A goal of economic life is to arrange location of factories and shops, the disposal of smoke and waste, the appearance of buildings and grounds, the use of science etc, so that the living environment will be healthy and aesthetically satisfying. The possible role of industry in creating aesthetical values is neglected aspect of political economy.

10. National Security: The goal of national security has become an importation pre-occupation of several countries. Economic activity is directly related to this goal because military power is based on the diversion of productive resources from circulation to military purposes.

11. Personnel Integrity: This economic goal is to maintain high standards of honour in all economic activities and transactions. This includes truthfulness in advertising and selling, observance of contract, fairness relations with competitors avoidance of questionable, financial manipulations, compliance it taxation, and general adherence to the rules of game, both in letter and in spirit.

Relationship between Social Responsibilities and Economic Growth

Some of the goals discussed above are found to be mutually conflicting in the sense that they attempt to achieve one of them may be at the sacrifice of another. Therefore, in applying these goals one has to compromise.

In general, the goals listed above are those by which the social performance of private, business is judged today. These are the goals which business men are expected t consider along with their own interests, when they are making decisions on production, prices, personnel, inventories, investment etc., it is suggested that the business man should assume responsibility to act in ways that will help in the achievement of economic goals. If they fail to do so organized society ceases to exist and chaos and anarchy prevails.

Social Responsibilities and Laissez Faire

One of the leading tenets of 18th century thought was that the pursuit of self interest by individuals is not always of necessarily anti social. Many intellectual leaders both in 18th and 19th centuries went for beyond the doctrine that the individual self interest and the social interest are not necessarily always inconsistent. They advanced the ideas that the untired pursuit of self interest would automatically lead to the best or most economical use of society's, productive resources.

It is true that the theory of Laissez Faire rested on certain conditions which have never being fully realized in practice' but the advocates of this doctrine believe that these conditions were reliable, at least to a degree, and that the principal arm of social economic policy lastly achieve them.

Classification of Social Responsibilities

In the fitness of the things the entire society can be divided into four groups:

1. Owners of business including shareholders of the company.
2. Workers.
3. Consumers,
4. Investment-the representative of the community.

1. Responsibility towards the owners of the business: Under the present companies Act, the shareholders possess four very important rights in addition to the fundamental right of speaking and voting at company meetings viz., 1. The right to pass the annual accounts, 2. Declare dividend.

3. Elect the directors of the company and 4. appointing the auditors of the company and fix their remuneration. Thus, in practice for the grant of a neatly it is very essential that the earnest effort to be made to develop shareholders opinion and they should be made to take an active interest in the working and management of the company.

2. *Responsibility Towards the workers*: It is necessary to keep the worker subscribed and give them their due share. This labour approach was looked down by the modern economists who land stress on the human approach. According to modern philosophy, labour in human being firs and work is next. What is actually required is employees representation in the Board of Directors.

3. *Responsibility Towards the Consumers*: The satisfaction of the consumes should be the primary concern of the business sector. Formation of the consumer councils should be given a sent in the Board of Directors. The consumers should be provided better and cheaper goals and it is responsibility to the business sector to fulfill their ambition.

5. *Responsibility towards government*: In order to serve the community before, Government shall have adequate funds. Taxation is a preferable means to secure the funds out of all the business a sets the individuals, firs and the corporate holders the companies are decidedly the class assets which can provide funds for he exchequer.

Social Responsibility projects:

The social responsibility projects are direct philosophy and indirect philosophy projects. One of the most frequently used projects for business is to try to mameliorate conditions. In decaying urban centres, populated by poor untranced individual who are often members of weaker sections and other minority groups. Business has been asked to do the following: (a) to hire and trying to do productive work (b) to set up and run job retraining centres to channel these people to other employers. (c) to provide public health information and education. (d) to locate new plants near the potential workers to purchase supplies from minority own business.

Environment Improvement Projects: These include city-run power plants, the automatic energy commission, nuclear programmes, nevertheless the environmental protection movement has asked for and received governmental support action designed to get business to clean up he environment.

10

Marketing Technology, Tasks, and Relationships

The possibilities of business expansion should also draw attention in market planning exercise. The implementation strategy, is then to be drawn based on the draft of marketing plan. The issues of distribution management, competitive pricing, qualitative dimensions of product, market information system, advertising strategy and effective sales approach form the core of implementation strategy. It is essential to review the extent of consumer satisfaction, demand and business performance, following the designed marketing plan and implementation strategy. These exercises comprise the core of monitoring and evaluation activity in the overall marketing management process.

The marketing system is a creation and reflection of our society, used to accomplish social as well as economic goals. Comparative marketing gains significance through recognition of its social and political aspects. Before a society can use marketing as a social tool, that society must undergo a transformation in which marketing evolves as a key institution. Specifically, several dimensions of marketing thought, the interdisciplinary approach, and the role of theory are discussed in this. Through integration of knowledge from such disciplines as mathematics, sociology, psychology, and philosophy the interdisciplinary approach to the study of marketing can help to develop and improve marketing judgement, comprehension, and practice. In the future, more attention should be focused on the development of marketing knowledge that will aid in explaining relationships and strengthen the foundation of marketing as a discipline. The development of marketing knowledge is not a simple process. The problem is one of achieving an understanding of relationships, structures, and patterns suggested by new information. This process is crucial to extending marketing thought, developing marketing as a science, and the fulfillment of marketing's broader roles.

That marketing is a tool has never been questioned. Whether it is a social and political tool, however, is a more profound proposition, particularly when this topic is related at the same time to "Ethical Considerations in Marketing" and to "Marketing: A Maturing Discipline." The implication is that because ethics is a consideration of the interrelated responsibilities of business and society, attention should be directed to the manner in which marketing is being used, as a tool, in fulfillment of its social responsibility. The extent of its attainment along this line is a measure of its maturity in the development from social irresponsibility toward social responsibility. That the discipline of marketing is maturing is evident even in the consideration of this topic, for twenty years ago it would not have been considered, and forty year ago there was even less concern with the social responsibility of marketing.

The question of whether marketing is a social and political tool appears on the surface to be a conclusive question, for which there may be a definite "yes" or "no" answer. Even a little consideration of it, however, suggests that it is a rhetorical or didactic question, one which serves better to evoke discussion than to make a definitive point. This is so because the question involves three or four concepts, all of which are still debatable than the terms of the title: "Marketing," "social," "tool." If this discussion can clarify these concepts, it will have made some contribution toward answering the question in issue.

Although marketing has now been studied for fifty or sixty years, students of the subject are more tentative in their definition of the term now than in the past. Originally, it was simply a practice, known s trade. Then it became a complex of considerations underlying the trading practice. Next it was viewed as the aggregate of functions for activities which serve as the means to an end. Thus, over the years, the concepts of marketing have been multiplied, diversified, and broadened, so that it is no longer merely the business tool, as originally conceived, but it, as implied by our topic, a social tool. Certainly that which was conceived as marketing when defined as a business tool could not be the object in thought when it is referred to as a social tool.

The maturing conception of marketing is a broadening one. Today it is regarded as asocial institution rather than merely a business institution of even primarily an economic institution. It is a comparative cultural means for society's attainment of some of its goals. That is to say that "marketing" designates n one society a means or institution which may be non-existent in another society, because either the latter's ends or means are different. Marketing is a particular type of societies' means of supplying the physical needs of its members. More precisely and elaborately stated, this concept implies that marketing is the means whereby society supplies its physical needs by the recognition and analysis of marketing the conception and promotion of marketable products, the physical distribution of them, and the transfer of their titles.

Returning to our original question, is marketing, so conceived, a social and political tool? From the sociological viewpoint, society is "an enduring, cooperative social group so functioning as to maintain itself and perpetuate the species." Society, therefore, embraces its institutions—including its political institution—through which it functions for the achievement of its goals. Thus society embraces and includes the economy, which serves but a particular type of social ends;

it includes the market, which may dominate and characterize the economy; it includes marketing, which is a more specialized institution within the market. In this sense, marketing is a social institution, a concept and creation of society, a medium sanctioned and ratified by society. From this viewpoint, society must be held embrace marketing, not marketing to embrace society.

The concept of a tool, in the sense of marketing as a tool, implies that it is an instrument or instrumentality employed for the achievement of certain effects. As such, it would be a means to an end. Can it be said that society uses as tools its institutions, such as marriage, religion, business, private property, credit, free enterprise, and the like?

Two views of this question are held. One is that society consists of its institutions and is not said to "use" them. Society is distinguished and characterized by its institutions, which are themselves the end manifestation of the values, ideals, and objectives of the society. The other is that society spawns and maintains its institutions not as manifestations of, but rather as means of achieving, its social values. In this sense, the marketing institution may be regarded as a tool used for the realization of such social ends as the following:

- Physical survival through he acquisition of the necessities of livelihood
- Equality of opportunity to consume
- Employment of specialized talents in specialized occupations
- Full utilization of extensive production capacity
- Freedom to negotiate
- Freedom to communicate, educate, and propagandize

"Marketing" is the term identifying the system by which our present society attempts to obtain these and other similar goals. Thus, broadly received, marketing is a social, including political, tool.

Simply to conclude that marketing is a social tool, however, does not warrant the inference that it is universally so used, or that where used it inevitably achieves desirable social results. With some justification, marketing may be regarded as a mature social phenomenon or, perhaps better, as a phenomenon of a mature society. Moreover, the ethical implications of marketing are inseparable from the ethics of society. To enlarge upon these points, let us consider some of the comparative, historical, and contemporary aspects of marketing.

Comparative Marketing

When it is recognized that marketing is a social institution, it will be acknowledged that the institution may vary indifferent societies. In some, which have not evolved the marketing concept, it may be non-existent. The potentiality of marketing as a social tool, therefore, is dependent upon the state or state of development of the society in which it appears. The study of marketing an institution relative to its social orientation is today known as Comparative Marketing, a subject of growing interest to students of marketing.

Eve a glance beyond the borders of the United States, the home of the original conception and development of marketing, shows the prevalence of marketing through out the world to coincide with the influence of Western business and, to some extent, with European colonization. Nations of so-called Western cultures have achieved the most advanced market economies and are making the most use of marketing as a social instrument, or tool, today. The underdeveloped countries—being not only underdeveloped in economic progress but culturally dissimilar from western society—make little use of marketing either as a social, economic or business tool. Those societies have not evolved in thought and practice the concept and institutions of marketing.

One of the significant discoveries concerning marketing during the last decade relating to this is the realization that marketing is not such a tool as can be imposed upon a society like a decree or mandate. Somewhat over-zealous governmental agents and American businessmen abroad have experienced the failure of the American marketing institution is countries to which it is unoriented. Similarly, some foreign aspirants to the achievements which out society has attained through the use of marketing have failed, for they have seen it only as a business tool and not as a social tool.

Before a society can use marketing—before this tool can be the instrumental of ethical or social responsibility to society—that society must undergo a transformation which evolves the institution of marketing. The following are some of the developments which must take place:

1. Consumer orientation of production and product planning. Although the market economy historically developed with production surpluses, until the viewpoint of production for the market is attained, the real significant of marketing is not recognized.

2. The conception of markets not as created by supply buts capable of expansion through demand creation. The effect of following tradition rather than promoting innovation in the market has produced unimaginativeness and hopelessness for gaining a higher standard of living. Even economists, minded by technological traditionalism, have under-estimated demand potentialities and limited their predictions of maximum markets. Holding a different view of this opens the way for marketing technology and an evolving marketing institution.

3. Profit motivation counteracting inertial in difference. Modern marketing cannot evolve where a business society prefers the leisure of low-volume mover with high markup to higher profits resulting from low markup and large volume.

4. Willingness to accept standardization and uniformity. The notion of real or fancied individualism in the

market, held by both distributors and consumers, prevents the use of techniques based upon concepts of mass consumption, mass distribution, and mass production, which are inherent in the modern marketing institution.

In other words, as society adopts attitudes and habits conducive to the development of marketing, it them finds contemporary marketing practices a tool for achieving social ends, in line with the adopted objectives.

The Tool in Contemporary American Society

The role which marketing has played and is playing in our contemporary society is inestimable. It has long been acknowledged as a business tool, an element in the management mix, a force for achieving corporate objectives, an means of imposing business standards upon the market. It is also an acknowledged economic tool—a solution for the disposition of production surpluses. An accelerating and a dynamic factor in the economy, a productive form of economic specialization. More than this, it is a social tool and is being used as such. Our marketing system is a social situation, a creation and reflection of our society, a highly complex and indicate mechanism or means used by society for the accomplishment not study of economic goals but also social objectives. The following are some of the ends attained by our society through the use of marketing:

1. The supplying of men's physical needs. Sociologists say that men have never lived self-sufficient unto themselves individually, but in all social systems either collective production, by such as the family or tribal group, or change has provided for the physical needs of men. We, today, are achievement this by the market economy and particularly by marketing.

2. Providing for a high degree of specialization of labour in society. Social economic theorists have long held that specialization or division of labour conducive to efficiency of performance. We today are dedicated to condu-

cive to efficiency of performance. We today are dedicated to deficiency as perhaps no other society has been. In consonance with this, though a great number of people are employed in marketing activity, this institution provides for not only regional and seasonal specialization in production, but also for specialized use of widely diversified talents in market activity.

3. Achieving a great diversity of products available for consumption. A criterion of status, standard of living and self preservation in our society is the diversity of products consumed. Marketing spreads at every doorstep a cornucopia of the world's luxuries, as well as the uncounted grades of a machine age. It is recognized, or course, that neither efficiency nor a plethora of things represents the social objective of some people. For them marketing is a less essential tool than for us.

4. Accelerating the rate of acquisition. Ours is an impatient society, whose market behavior seems to enact the philosophy that "it's later than you think." What might be acquired in the near or distant future is wanted today. Marketing, particularly through the instrument of credit, is used to make this possible.

5. Defining of a concept of fairness in society. Every society has its ethics, its codes of relationships, obligations, and values, and by custom or law these standards are spelled out. Our own ethical judgments have evolved with the growth of our society; and these principles have found expression, in part, in many regulations of marketing practice, thereby using he institution of marketing for the preservation of social values.

6. Shifting responsibilities for consumer decision-making to technical specialists. With economic specialization, consumption has taken ion a distinct character. Te function of planning the products to be used has been shifted to producers. The maintenance of supplies available for consumption has been shifted to retailers and wholesal-

ers. By our policies relating to returns, adjustment, and guarantees, purchasing is not completed at the time of transaction but at an indefinite later time, as through the tool of marketing society achieves an objective of shifted responsibility.

7. Creating uniformity of living standards. Through marketing, by which almost all types of products are made available and accessible at many locations, a great mass market has been created, and an economic manifestation of our social concept of equality among men has been achieved. Our society's praise of democratic and religious equalization has found expression through the tool of marketing.

8. Achieving cultural integration among nations as the institution of marketing is introduced. Notwithstanding the fact that marketing is an institution which societies evolve, in this era marketing is also used a means by which its underlying social values are taught to people with differing social structures, volumes and customs. Whereas in times past colonizers and economic frontiersmen introduced corn see, tobacco, or cattle stock for the development of a primitive economy, now cultural hybridarise is undertake by the introduction of marketing concepts and techniques. For example, the Swiss Migros chain of food stores has recently authored use of its name trademarked merchandise. And operating methods in Spain aid the development of voluntary chains there and to extend company protection. Likewise, the opening of American type consumer loan companies in Latin American and European cities will also teach the commercialization of confidence, the impersonalization of borrowing, and the supervised of legal commercial practices to unregulated and illegal forms of lending.

9. Expressing society's changing sense of values.

In summary, as Shakespeare admonished the players in Hamlet, "To told, as 'twere, the mirror up to nature; to show virtue her own feature, born her own image, and the very age and body of the time his form and pressure," so marketing mirrors the society in which it has evolved and is practiced. It is social tool, and, as such, it is as laudable as the society which employs it is good.

Societal Impact on Consumers

The marketing concept is philosophy of service and mutual gain. However, all marketers do not follow the marketing philosophy. Some companies use questionable marketing practices which affect the larger society. Take the case of cigarettes. A company is free to sell cigarette and smokers are free to buy them. But this transactions is harmful to public interest. First, the smoker is shortening his own life. Second, other people around the smoker have to inhale the smoke and suffer discomfort and harm. Marketing managers should be aware of the main criticisms of marketing. Certain marketing practices hurt individual consumers, society as a hole and other business firms. Consumers surveys show that consumers hold unfavourable attitudes towards marketing practices. Consumers are most worried about high prices, poor quality and dangerous or unsafe products, misleading advertising claims and poor service to consumers.

Critics point out that consumers are hard hit because prices are higher because high cost of distribution, high advertising and promotion cots and excessive mark-ups. Critics charge that greedy middlemen mar up prices beyond the value of their services. There are too many middlemen and they provide unnecessary or duplicate services. As a result, distribution costs are too much and consumers pay for these excessive costs in the shape of higher prices.

The retailers answer this criticism by saying that rising mark up reflects improved services, that consumers themselves want—more convenience, larger stores, longer store hours, return privileges and soon. Moreover, the cots of operating stores keep on rising, forcing retailers to raise their prices.

Secondly, modern marketing is accused of pushing up prices because of heavy advertising and sales promotion. Differentiated products—cosmetics, toiletries—include promotion and packaging costs that might amount to 40% of the manufacturer's price to the retailer.

Marketers answer these charges by saying that consumers want more thanthe merely functional qualities of products. They also want psychological benefits—they want to feel wealthy, beautiful or special. Consumers usuallycanbuyfuncitonal versions of products of lower prices but often are willing to pay more for products that also provide desired psychological benefits. Second, branding gives buyers confidence. A brand name implies a certain quality and consumers are willing to pay for well known brands even if they cost a little more. Third, heavy advertising is needed to inform millions of potential buyers of the merits of a brand. It consumers want to know what is available on the market, they must expect manufacturers to spend a lot of money on advertising.

Critics also charge that some companies mark up goods excessively, expecially in the drug industry. Marketers respond that most businesses try to deal fairly with consumers because they want repeat business. Most consumer abuses are unintentional. Marketers argue that pharmaceutical markets must cover the costs of purchasing, promoting and distributing existing medicines plus high research and development costs of finding new medicines.

Marketers sometimes are accused of deceptive practices. Consumers do not got what they expect. Deceptive practices fall into three groups—deceptive pricing, promotion and packaging. Deceptive pricing includes practices such as overstanding the product's features, luring the customers to he store for a bargain that is out of stock. Deceptive packaging includes exaggerating package contents through subtle design, not filling the package to the top or using misleading labeling. Deception practices have led to consumer protection actions.

Marketers argue that most companies avoid deceptive practices because such practices harm their business in the long run. If consumers do not get what they expect, they will switch to more reliable products.

Salespeople are sometimes accused of higher pressure selling hat persuades people to buy goods they had no thought of buying. It is often said that jewelry, insurance and encyclopaedias are sold, not bought. Salesmen are trained to deliver smooth talks to entice purchase. Marketers know that buyers often buy unwanted things because undue selling pressure has been applied.

Consumers often criticize that products lack the quality they should have. It is complained that products are not made well. It is also complained that some products deliver little benefit. Many of the "healthy" foods being sold in the market may have no nutritional value; they may be even harmful. It is also complained that companies are selling unsafe products.

Marketing Impact on Society

It is alleged that the marketing system put too much interesting material possessions. People are judged by what they own rather than by what they are. Traditional Indian values have gone. Money is the incantation of today. Too much interest in material things is not a natural state of mind but rather a matter of false wants created by marketing. Business uses the mass media to create materialistic models of the good life. People work harder to earn the necessary money. Their purchases increase the output of our industry and industry in turn stimulate more desire for the industrial output. Thus, marketing is seem as creating false wants that benefit industry more than they benefit consumers.

However, these criticisms exaggerate the power of business to create needs. People have strong defences against advertising and other marketing tools. Marketers are most effective when they appeal to existing wants rather than when they attempt to create new ones. Moreover, people seek information when making important purchases and often do not rely on single sources. A high failure rate of new products shows the companies are not able to control demand.

Basically our wants and values are influenced not only by marketers but also by family, peer groups, religion, ethnic background and education. If people are highly materialistic, these values arose out of basic socialization processes that go much deeper than business and mass media could produce alone.

Business in criticized of overselling private goods at the expense of public goods. A private goods increase, they require more public services which are not forthcoming. For example, an increase in car ownership (private good) requires more highways, traffic control and parking spaces (Public goods). The overselling of private goods results in social cost. Incase of automobiles, social costs include air pollution, traffic congestion and deaths from car accidents. A balance had to be restored between private ad pubic goods. One method would be to ask producers bear the full social costs of their operations.

Cultural Pollution: the marketing system is criticized for creating cultural pollution. Our senses are being assaulted constantly by advertising. Pages of ads obscure printed matter billboards mar beautiful scenery. These commercials pollute people's minds with messages of materialism, sex, power or status. Markets answer the charges of "commercial noise" with these arguments. First, they hope that their ads reach mainly the target audience. Some ads are bound to reach people through mass communication channels who have no interest in the product and are annoyed. Second, ads keep down the cost of magazines and newspapers.

It is alleged that a company's marketing practices can hard other companies and reduce competition.

Critics charge that firms are harmed and competition reduced when companies expand by acquiring competitors rather than by developing their own products. Acquisition is not always bad, it may be good for society. The acquiring company may gain economies of scale that lead to lower costs and lower prices. A well-managed company may take over a poorly managed company and improve its efficiency. An industry that was not very competitive become more competitive after acquisition. But as acquisition might be harmful, government regulation is necessary.

Critics also accuse that marketing practices, prevent new companies from entering an industry. Large marketing companies can use parents and heavy promotion spending and tie up dealers to drive out competitors.

Finally, some companies have used unfair competitive marketing practices with the intention of destroying others. They may set their prices below costs and discourage the buying of a competitor's products.

Some people think that business is the cause of many social ills. The two major movements have taken place to keep business in line. The basic idea behind the consumer movement is protection of the right of consumers. This movement started in USA. The first movement which took place in 1900s, was sparked by rising prices. The second movement was sparked by rising consumer prices during the Great Depression. The third movement took place in 1960s. It was Ralph Nader who appeared on the scene and accused big businesses of wasteful and unethical practices.

Consumerism or consumer movement is an organized movement of citizens and government agencies. Traditional sellers' rights include:

The right to introduce any product in any size and style, provided it is not hazardous to personal health or safety or it is, to include proper warnings and controls.

* The right to charge any price for the product.

* The right to spend any amount to promote the product.

* The right to use any product message provided it is not misleading or dishonest.

* The right to use any buying incentive schemes, provided they are not unfair or misleading.

Traditional buyers' rights include:

(i) The right not to buy a product that is offered for sale.

(ii) The right to expect the product to be safe.

(iii) The right to expect the product to perform as claimed.

Comparing these rights, it is believed that the balanced of power lies on the sellers' side. The buyer can refuse to buy no doubt. But the buyer actually has too little education, information and protection to make wise decisions when facing powerful sellers. The consumer wants the following additional consumer rights.

(1) The right to be well in forced about the important aspects of the product.

(2) The right to be protected against questionable products and marketing practices.

(3) The right to influence products and marketing practices in ways that will improve the "quality of life".

It was President Kennedy who declared the consumers' rights for the first time in his message to the American Congress in March, 1962. They were the right to information, the right to choose and the right to be heard. Later, International Organization of consumers' Union added four more rights, i.e., the right to redress, the right to consumer education, the right to healthy environment and the right to basic needs. These rights were incorporated in the United Nations' Charter of Human Rights. The Government of India also recognized these rights later.

The consumer movement exercises a considerable influence on the socioeconomic environment of business. In a country like India where there is a high percentage of illiteracy among people, where people are less informed and where critical goods are always in short supply, the government has a significant role in safeguarding the interests of consumers by promoting a climate of fair competition and preventing exploitation of consumers. For many centuries there are dictum Caveat Emptor—buyers beware. The consumer movement has changed it and sellers feel now it is a question of sellers beware. The objective of the consumer movement is to secure the interests of the consumer against al types of unfair trade practices. Consumerism as an effective and organized movement started in 1960s in the USA. Ralph Nader has lifted consumerism into a major social force. Consumerism may be defined as a social force within the environment designed to aid and protect the consumers by exerting legal, moral and economic pressures on business and government.

The consumer movement highlights the following four fundamental rights of consumers.

1. Right to safety to be protected against the marketing of goods which hare hazardous to health or life.

2. Right to be Informed to be protected against fraudulent, deceitful or grossly misleading information, advertising labeling or other practices and to be given the facts needed to make an informed choice.

3. Right to Choose to be assured access to a variety of products and services at competitive prices and in those industries in which Government regulations are substituted, to be assured satisfactory quality and service at fair price.

4. Right to be Heart to be assured that consumer interests will receive full and sympathetic consideration in the formulation of Government policy and fair and expeditious treatment in its administrative tribunals.

The following features of consumer movement are noteworthy:

1. It is basically a protest movement.
2. It is a mass movement in the sense that masses are the general body of consumers.
3. It is generally a non-official movement. Public and voluntary consumers' organizations initiate the movement.
4. Tough it is not a government-sponsored movement, it is recognized and backed up by the Government.

In a *laissezs-faire* society, consumer was a king and he was free to choose. But the consumer sovereignty is a myth and the supposed benefit to the consumer accruing from perfect competition has not realized. The actual world is a world of imperfect or monopolistic competition and the consumer has only a limited amount of freedom in making purchase choices. When the consumer will be able to asset himself, 'the take it or leave if' nature of transaction sin the Indian market will end. As the manufacturer has the free choice to produce and sell his goods so the consumer should have the free choice to select from the range\of products available. This is what is meant by consumer's sovereignty in the present socio-economic context.

Consumers as a class in our country are the only group of people who are so disorganized that they are being exploited al the time by other sectors of the economy—industry, labour and agriculture. Indian consumer is confronted with foodstuff and goods that are adulterated, substandard and unsafe, price that are inflated and weights and measures that perennially short-change him. We do not agree with Prof. Samuelson when he says that business of business is business. Business is not an island in itself. It is part and parcel of society as a whole. Hence it should be constantly alive and alert to the responsibilities to the society. Consumer protection movement is an attempt to make the businessmen aware of their social responsibilities.

Some legislative measures have already been taken by the Government to safeguard the interests of the Indian consumer. There are a wide range of enactments which operate to protect the consumer. The agricultural Produce (Grading and Marketign0 act, 1937 constitutes the basic law for the grading of agricultural produce. The Drugs and Cosmetics Act, 1940 regulates the import, manufacture, sale and distribution of drugs and cosmetics. The Prevention of Food Adulteration Act, 1959 aims at preventing the sale of impure foodstuff. The Essential Commodities Act, 1955, regulates the production, supply, distribution and trade in essential commodities and securing equitable distribution and availability at fair prices. The Packaged Commodities (Regulation) Order, 1979, requires manufacturers to display on labels and packages the weight, contents of the product, date of manufacture, selling price and address of the manufacturer. Some other important acts include the Display of Price Order, 1973, the Drugs and Magic Remedies (objectionable advertisement Act, 1954, and the Cigarettes (Regulation of production, Supply and Distribution) Act, 1975. Lately the Government has enacted the Consumer Protection Act, 1986. Through this Act, an attempt has been made to strengthen the institutional framework to protect the consumer at local, state and central level.

There are various institutional factors which are responsible for growing concern for the consumer protection in India. To begin with, the Government is anxious to protect the vulnerable sectors of the community though schemes like streamlining the public distribution system. Owing to inflation, different anti-social elements have appeared in the market place for exploiting the poor consumers through unfair trade practices like adulteration, underweight, substandard products or goods in short supply. Hence the Government has come forward to protect the consumers through the Maintenance of Internal Security Act., MRPT Act., 1969 and the Consumer Protection Act, 1986.

Secondly, the Indian traders did not bother about a consumers because there had been a sellers' market. Today the market environment for most products has changed. Now it is a buyers' market. Unless the consumers are protected against dishonest and unethical business practices, the long-run business interest will suffer. Now the business community is becoming aware of the social responsibility towards customers.

Thirdly, the consumers are becoming more and more conscious of their rights and legitimate demands. The present day consumers are not ignorant of the market environment. They are conscious of customers' rights and to protect their interest, they form organizations lie consumer Co-operative and Consumers' Councils.

Lastly, the consumer burden imposed by the government is on the increase. On the pretext of fiscal discipline, the tax burdens are increased every year. It has almost become a practice to announce pre-budget hike in administered prices like petro-products, railway fares and post and telegraph rates. It I quite natural that there will be consumers' resistance to these additional burdens.

In India consumerism is still in its infancy although the consumers suffer from exaggerated advertisements, impure quality of products, under-weights, high prices and artificial scarcity of many essential articles. Though some consumer organizations have been set up in different part of the country, the movement has yet to gather sufficient strength to become a living force to reckon with.

There are many hindrances to the growth of a strong consumer movement in India.

First, there is lack of leadership and management, In India, there is no Ralph Nader who can give a dynamic leadership to this movement. Secondly, the majority of the people are illiterate. They lack consumer education and do not have the necessary consciousness to organize themselves. Thirdly, India is a vast country and it is very difficult to have quick, effective and regular communication among different parts of the country. Different languages and different customers different regions hamper he growth of the movement. Fourthly, to\organize the consumer movement throughout the country needs huge financial resources. Lack of financial resources is a handicap to the growth of the movement.

Lastly, the attitude of people is not favourable to the growth of a consumer movement in India. There is a tendency among the people to look to the government for protection and assistance rather than to stand on their own legs and put up resistances. Till recently, apart from the legal measures, the main planks for protecting consumers have been the public distribution system and consumer cooperative movement. Public distribution system started during the Second. World War and it is now in operation in the case of consumer goods. It covers foodgrains, sugar, kerosene and controlled cloth. The fifth plan proposed to expand the coverage to include pulses ad edible oil. It was intended to keep prices in check and to ensure equitable distribution of scarce but basic foods. The system also helped to check hoarding and black marketing. The public distribution system does not necessarily improve the distribution of income but it helps to prevent a deterioration in distribution in inflationary conditions. Shortages of essential goods as well as inflation can be highly regressive if a public distribution system does not prevent serious cuts in the consumption of the poor.

Through the prices of essential items such as cereals bought form the fair price shops have been lower than prices in the open market, but the quality is substandard and the quantity insufficient. The poor are often unable to buy their requirements from the fair price shops because they do not have cash in hand. They usually go to private traders who provide credit facility even fit means actually paying a much higher price. Sine most of the unfair trade practices are due to shortage in supply, what is needed is a rapid increase in production of all varieties of consumer goods and quality, price and distribution would take care of themselves.

The National Consumer Protection Council under theChairmanshp of the Union Minister of Civil Supplies and Co-operation has bene established to promote and develop consumer movement throughout the country. The Council will inform itself fully about consumers' problems, collect and disseminate information relating to consumer matters, assist the state-governments in development of consumer movement, examine consumer grievances and initiate remedial action and promote equitable distribution of mass consumption commodities at fair prices.

Environmentalists consider the effect of marketing system on the environment and with the costs of serving consumer needs and wants. They are concerned with damage to the ecosystem caused by strip mining, forest depletion, acid rain, loss of the atmosphere's ozone layer, toxic wastes and littler. They are also worried with the loss of recreational areas and with the increase in health problems caused by bad air, polluted water and chemically treated food. There are the major concerns of citizens and government agencies and they want to protect and improve people's living environment. Environmentalists are not against marketing, what they want is that organizations should operate with more care of or the environment. The goal of marketing system should be not to maximize consumption but to maximize quality of life. Quality of life not only means the quality and quantity of consumer goods and services but also the quality of the environment. Environmentalists want environmental costs included in both producer and consumer decision making.

Environmentalism has hard hit some industries. Steel companies and public utilities have to spend huge amount of money for pollution-control programmes. The auto-industry has had to introduce expensive emission controls in cards. The packaging industry has had to find ways to reduce litter. The gasoline industry has had to created new no-lead gas lines. These companies have absorbed large costs and have passed them on to buyers.

Environmentalism has created problems for marketers. They have to raise prices to cover environmental costs, knowing that it would be difficult to sell the products. The protection of the natural environment would be the major issue for people in the 21 century. Companies are responding with 'green marketing"—developing ecologically safer products, recyclable and biodegradable packaging better pollution controls and more energy-efficient operations. But now most companies accept new consumer right. Many of them have responded positively to consumerism and environmentalism in order to serve consumer needs better.

The philosophy of enlightened marketing holds that a company's marketing should support the long-run interest of the marketing system. Enlighted marketing involves five principles—consumer-oriented marketing, innovative marketing, value marketing, sense-of-mission marketing and societal marketing.

Consumer-oriented marketing means that the company should look at marketing activities from the consumer's point of view. It should work hard to sense, serve and satisfy the needs of a particular group of customers. The principles of innovative marketing requires that the company is continuously marking marketing improvements. The company that ignores new and better ways of doing business will eventually lose customers. According to the principle of value marketing, the company should put most of its resources not value-building marketing investments. Enlightend marketing demands building long-run consumer loyalty by continuously improving the value consumers received form he firm's marketing offer.

Sense-of-marketing means that the company should define its mission in broad social terms rater than narrow product term. According to the principle of societal marketing, an enlightened company makes marketing decisions by considering consumers' wants and long-run interest, company's requirements and society's long-run interests. The company knows that neglecting society' long-run interest is a positive disservice to the society. Societal problems should be looked upon as opportunities. Products can be classified according to their degree of immediate consumer satisfaction and long-run benefits. Desirable products give both high immediate satisfaction and high long-run benefits. Pleasing products give high immediate satisfaction but may hurt consumers in the long run.

Marketing as a Social Process

To an increasing extent, marketing is conceived as a social process, the purpose of which is the identification and the satisfaction of the wants of customers. When so viewed as a social process concerned with want satisfaction, marketing is readily identified as a subject of much broader scope than the compilation of functions or activities commonly identified as marketing responsibilities in individual companies.

Most here present will accept this view, but nevertheless there are many teachers in the room who very recently were using textbooks, or there relying upon the AMA glossary of terms, that defined marketing as the performance of business activities that direct the flow of goods and services from producers to consumer or user." Recognition that marketing is indeed a social process that extends far beyond the business activities of individual participants operating within the process is indeed a considerable advance. It gives to marketing a dynamic quality and a sense of purpose that was more often lacking under the common concept of getting goods from production to consumption.

Yet, whether we be educators or practitioners, in espousing marketing as a social process concerned with the ant satisfaction of consumers, were may have inadvertently exaggerated the consumer-oriented nature of marketing. From much of the recent literature, including some of my own, one might well get the impression that marketing consists mostly of business firms finding nice things to do for people. However, much of what actually goes on under the guise of marketing in our present social system has nothing to do with the wants of people, except in the most broad and general sense if even the n we can attribute decisions of politicians and government administrators to a reflection of the will of the people. To do so is certainly tenuous, for who can say that consumers can even comprehend, yet alone desire, the pressured values of being first on the moon, of having concrete rather than asphalt highways, of rushing to provide more facilities for higher education, of rebuilding the core of cities through urban renewal programmes, or of having planes built by General Dynamics rather than by Boeing, Similarly, a decision on the part of a public electric utility to construct a large new power plant rather than to purchase energy from others for distribution may have substantial marketing impact in industry, although changing in no appreciable way the values sought or received by consumers, as may also be the case when aluminum rather than stainless steel is specified to sheathe frame of a new office building.

There is another defect in the concept of marketing as a social process concerned with the identification and satisfaction of customer wants. The concept as commonly stated assumes that marketing is an adaptive process in our culture. In accordance with this view, it is generally assumed of stated that the firm is adjusting its product offer to market requirements which it has discovered by marketing research approaches. While this may ell be true, when viewed from the standpoint of any one manufacturer of perfume coffee, or cigarettes, the aggregate social impact of all marketing activity is, in my judgment, commonly underestimated, especially by those in the marketing field.

Marketing Technology, Tasks, and Relationships

Marketing technology which is applicable to a process, or is it a process in which marketing technology is one of several guides to action. This is not a semantical question.

It is a proposition with significance of marketing practioners and theoreticians alike.

Stated otherwise: Is marketing the knowledge and practice of technical laws and precepts, the actions of individuals, a micro-phenomenon in a world of business? Or is it a process more broadly conceived, involving a society of actions, one guide to which is knowledge of market and marketing behaviour?

Evidence of such a divergence of viewpoints appeared as early as the 1980s both in marketing theory—with integrative expositions differing term traditional functional-institutional analyses—and in marketing practice—with traditional profit factors as a sole guide to marketing action making supplemented by reciprocal interests in the seller-buyer and seller-public dyads.

So marked have these differences become in recent years that academics and their programmes have been identified with one or the other concept; and business concerns have been characterized by the extent to which they rejected or accepted consumer-orientation, social responsibility, and international behaviour.

While divergent viewpoints are wholesome in a growing discipline, sooner or later the integration of them in a unified statement is desirable. Seldom is this the work of any one individual but more often a gradual clarification of concepts and issues.

Historical Perspectives

Appraisal of the current status of marketing must be made in terms of its history. Thus, one looks to evolution in social change as the nutriment of change in marketing practice and theory. Successive tasks imputed to marketing impelled the emergence of the traditional functional-institutional approach to marketing, the managerial decision-making approach the behhavioristic or inter-disciplinary approach, and the quantitative statement of marketing variables.

The formulation of this branch of knowledge is for purposes of action in business situations—particularly for the making of administrative decisions by individuals engaged in marketing. While this is often termed "Marketing management" or "managerial decision-making," neither formerly nor currently have all marketing decisions been made on the "managerial" level in businesses. Some have been made below that level some above.

Moreover, many marketing decisions are made outside the formal organization for management in the business establishment—such s those made by consumers, by governmental agencies, by the general public, and by informal organizations of business entrepreneurs.

The real issue is: What kinds of knowledge for what kinds of action?

Marketing Technology

The sum of marketing knowledge has been variously designated—as a "science," an "art," and a "discipline." There is justification for considering also another term in connection with marketing, namely, technology –marketing technology.

Te concept of marketing knowledge as a technology has some useful implications. Marketing practice developed as a technique; marketing thought developed as a technology.

Technique was the preoccupation of practitioners. Technology the concern of marketing scholars, who in addition to the description conceptualization, and synthesis of prevailing techniques undertook to rationalize, interpret, account for, and appraise them.

All of the circumstances which gave rise to marketing called for a technology. At the turn of this century there was practically no systematic knowledge of he processes of business sin the marketplace.

Economic theory provided no guidance for individual

behaviour in distribution; it has been conceived as general economic analysis rather than as working technology. Moreover, even if it had, the changing circumstances of production, distribution consumption, and changes in the state of the arts, social values, attitudes, and practices at that time called for new actions and new guides to action.

Prominent among the problems of that day were the stimulation of consumption in a growing buyers' market, the pricing of products in new multi-channel systems of distribution, the appraising of credit applications in evolving credit economy, and the like.

The outcome of this need was a mélange of ideas which became known "marketing"—a combination of borrowings form economics, psychology, management theory, and original findings. "Marketing" came to designate both technique and technology.

Throughout ensuring years the questions have been even more significant: Is marketing the core of concept which are uniquely characteristic of this area of inquiry and behaviour—the marketing technology? Or is it the broad inclusion of all types of concepts and findings, drawn from a variety of disciplines? And if it is the latter, where is the line to differentiate marketing from other area of though.

Close scrutiny of marketing thought discloses that it has generally dealt either with nonhuman aspects of human behaviour in distribution, or with individual behaviour in the process of distribution. It scarcely need be said and people use marketing ecnique, and that marketing technology describes the techniques of an interpersonal process.

However, the contents of marketigntraditionally have bene concerned primarily with the nonhuman and impersonal:

Nonhuman:

Economic concepts—Price, costs, profits, margins, turnover

Space-time elements—Location, layout Processes—

Selling, buying, financing Intangibles—Brands, images, policies

Objects—Product classes, consumer types

Impersonal:

Institutions—Wholesalers, retailers, producers, government

Collectives—Markets, credit risks, competitors.

The circumstances which evoked this technology called for guides to in marketing relationships; but the actual behaviour of individuals in the relationships was little considered.

There were several reasons. Human behaviour was taken to be what, in classical economic concepts of man, it was assumed to be. Market behaviour was assumed to conform to patterns of the economic man and the regulatory government. Business was synonymous with management; and one viewpoint, a managerial viewpoint, was paramount Management was dominant. Success varied with the application of techniques, the flow of influence being outward and unidirectional from management. Moreover, the mechanics of the firm subordinated individual identities within it.

There are several advantages to regarding marketing thought as a technology. It assists in differentiating the technology of marketing from other business technologies—such as those of manufacturing, agriculture, finance, accounting, and law. It differentiates marketing also from other social disciplines which are not business technology, but which have contributed to business and marketing thought—economic theory, sociology, anthropology, psychology, political theory, etc. It identifies that segment of thought in which marketing specialists are presumed to be responsible for original and creative thinking—that segment of though which is essential in a marketing curriculum..

Contents of Marketing Technology

The technology itself consists mainly of concepts and

of relationships among variables. The main categories of thought are derivations of a concept of the marketing task or process, of which there are several—distributing products, performing functions, managing institutions or organizations involved in distribution, serving markets to be supplied.

Its categories reflect, too, several concepts form the economics of the firm—profit-motivation, specialization and integration; economies of scale or operation; and variability of costs. They represent marketing as a technical, mechanistic procession a non-technical, social environment, in which consumer and government behaviour are recognized at least to be affected by many non-economic factors.

Thus, the framework of marketing typically has consisted of the concepts and principles implicit in the process of distributing goods and transferring title to them, as marketing has generally been defined. Its principal structural elements have been these:

- Market research, delimitation, segmentation
- Product conception, adaptation, identification, diversification
- Functional performance, including demand creation
- Institutional specialization and channel composition
- Price-cost-profit relationships in internal and external management decisions
- Market and marketing finance
- Social regulation of marketing

Throughout its history the technology of marketing thought has provided a guide for action on several management and operational levels. But this technology has been generally used as though action were simply rather than an interaction—as though it were a guide mainly for the achievement of self-determined corporate goal, rather than of the interrelated expectations of a number of participants in the marketing process.

Marketing as a Social Process

It is generally conceded that marketing is a process, but there often is agreement as to what kind of a process it is. Traditionally it has been regarded as a managerial process and as an economic process. The former embodies the application of a marketing technology: the latter assumes economic behaviourism.

Cross-cultural ad comparative marketing studies, however, along with increasing pollination of marketing thought with sociological concepts, have shown marketing to be also a social process. That phrase has meant to some marketing teachers and practitioners only that social circumstances of consumers, other than those that are economic, must be taken into consideration in planning marketing strategy.

More broadly considered, the process of marketing is social, in that it is a process whereby society is fulfilling the personal and institutional needs of the society for physical or consumption goods and services. Every society is supplying this common need of its members through means that are similar or dissimilar –depending on the character, organization, objectives, and technologies of the particular society.

Marketing as Social Interaction

Marketing is a process not merely of action but of Interaction. It is not merely what is done by wholesalers, retailers, producers, and others as separate and discrete economic or social entities.

Rather, it I the action and interaction of people (not as wholesalers. But as people) in the broad process of economic want-fulfillment.

Although a wholesale establishment is a technical or mechanistic specialist performing assembly ad redistribution and operating under the technology of the economics of the firm it is, socially viewed, some individual acting in the role of management.

From the standpoint of his retail customer, he is acting in the role of resource or supplier; from the standpoint of the original producer, he is acing in he role of an intermediate customer. The person acting as a wholesaler does not act wholly as an economic man; and therefore the traditional technology, based upon the assumption that he does, cannot fully explain or provide a guide for his actions.

Marketing Tasks and Roles

As a social process, marketing in its entirety constitutes the sets of relationships which arise in the performance of the process of economic want-satisfaction. In our consumer-oriented, profit-motivated, market guided, entrepreneur-initiated, government-regulated society, ten participating business role positions are identifiable:

Manager	intermediate customer
Employee	resource
Owner	competitor
Other investor	government
Consumer	community

Marketing is the process of interaction among these sets or systems of relationships.

Of course, marketing has not always consisted of this full range of roles, nor have their relative positions always been the same. Throughout the 19th century and during the early formative years of the study marketing in this century, the owner and manager roles (sometimes combined, and sometimes separated) constituted the sole or principal relationship. Management assumed no other responsibilities, as is evidenced by such concepts as "laissez faire," "caveat emptor," and "Social Darwinism." Guides to behaviour were mainly profit guides; and the task of marketing was to make a profit.

When in 1890 a new dimension was given to management in the Sherman Act, and thereafter in subsequent marketing legislation, the role of the competitor became more of a factor in management. With labour legislation in the 1920s, the relations of management to employees became more prominent.

Similarly, with the "consumer movement" the role of the consumer was emphasized.

In subsequent years the roles of government, investors, and the community became more prominent; and with each successive addition the ask of management in the marketing process has become increasingly complex.

The task of marketing management today is not merely to run the mechanism of a marketing establishment, but also to coordinate and to balance the expectations of individuals in their various roles. In performing this function as a social-role participant, management today has a different and vastly more complex obligation than some years ago. Prominent among the guides to action is the whole body of marketing technology to which we have been referring.

However, the important distinction between marketing past and marketing to come is the fact that hereafter one will be less likely to confine this competence simply to a knowledge of "Marketing"—marketing technology—as thought solitary action within this framework were the attainment of the ultimate.

Rather, the marketing manager of tomorrow—recognizing hi position a social role in social process wherein he and all whom he contacts are resumed to be social rather than mere economic or technical entities—regard marketing technology simply as one of several tools to guide as to what is "right' and "wrong" to do in the marketing process.

This accentuates rather than diminishes the imperative for him to know marketing technology. To define marketing as a technical, mechanistic, or managerial process emphasizes technology, economic behaviour, and conventional marketing "principles." To define it as a behavioural process emphasizes non-economic, non-business motivations, and human behaviour patterns. To define it as a social process emphasizes the cultural orientation of business in relation to other social institutions, organisations, and values.

11

Organisational Implications of the Modern Marketing Concept

Modern marketing is both a philosophical and an organizational concept. As a philosophy, the modern marketing concept recognizes that the customer is king; that a business entity's only purpose for existence is to service the customer; and that all commercial activity must begin with a determination of the customer's wants and desires and end with a fulfillment of them in most expeditious and efficient manner. Inherent in this philosophy is existence of a truly customer-conscience organization embracing all personnel from the lowest operating level to the president. Indelibly imprinted on each employee's mind must be the dictum: "We are forever beholden to the customer."

But a company cannot become customer conscious by edict. Since the organizations tend to emulate their leader, it is most important that the head of the business be thoroughly customer conscious. There can only be one marketing head in any business and that must be the president. It can develop a mood, an atmosphere, and an esprit de corps reflecting the pre-eminence of the customer that permeates every nook and corner the company.

The best evidence of a truly customer-conscious company is that it in intimately acquainted with the customers' business. A market-oriented company acts anal thinks in terms of the final end use of its product, raw materials, parts, or sub-assemblies. For example, the fertilizer business not just concerned with selling fertilizers, it is involved in growing food. Therefore, it is necessary for fertilizer manufacturers to understand the farmer, in all of his requirements, to be in a better position to serve distributors who must ultimately appeal to farmers for the sale of fertilizer.

While this philosophical view is an essential prerequisite to success marketing it must be supplemented by a strong organizational approach. For in addition to being customer conscious and market oriented company must also organize and programme marketing activities to provide the customer with adequate products and services. This is probably the weakest link in the marketing activities of most companies. Company may have the will and the desire to serve the customer, but all too of they are inadequately organized to do so.

Proper organization must result in a total integration and coordination of all of the factors that can influence the final sale. This is the every essence of the modern marketing concept. If advertising, direct selling merchandising, transportation, publicity, and the other ales influences treated as separate entities, and are autonomously executed, their respective contributions are fairly well vitiated. When they are integrated in the completely coordinated communications programme, the total impact greatly compounded.

Managers sped a very high proportion of their time not only with their subordinates, but also with their superiors and their equals and as well as with a great range of individuals outside the firm. No single definition discussed in the above paragraphs touches the entirety of the essence of management. But a very comprehensive definition was given by a team of academicians of the United States business schools in around 1940. the team aimed at deciding a definition that businessmen would accept and practice and that academician would teach. According to that team: "Management is guideline human and physical resources into dynamic organization units that attain their objective to the satisfaction of those served and with a high degree of morale and sense attainment on part of those rendering the service". According to this definition management consists the following five ingredients. Management involves guiding human and physical resources. A manager must balanced between these two resources. He can not put more emphasis on physical resources and ignore human resources or vice-versa. He should not neglect people over technology. There should be equal concern for human and as well as physical resources.

Nature of the Organisation

The environment in which organizations are existing is dynamic. The environment is subject to change which brings stress on organisations. For example changes in technology, market condition, competitive products and services, attitudes of customers demands the organization to adapt timely measures to achieve there determined goal. Managers must e competent to predict in advanced of these changes so as to make able the organization to readily adapt to such changes in the environment. Such organizations are said to be dynamic. Thus management make organization to become dynamic.

Attainment of predetermined objective will be the ultimate goal of the organization which should be accomplished by the management. The purpose of the organization should not be lost. Goat realization is the mission of the management. Goals may differ from organization to organisation but the takes of management is to reach such goals.

The performance in regard to attainment of objectives can be measured through the degree of satisfaction derived by those who are served. The public or the consumers are the people who are served by the organisations. Hence the consumer satisfaction should be he prime concern of the management. Management can become successful only through attaining consumer satisfaction.

This segment of the definition refers to members of employees of and organisation. It is the management's responsibility to see that all the employees are happy with the organisation. The level of their morale, and sense of belongingness to organisation strongly influence the success of the organisation. Because the kind of satisfaction derived from their work will have impact on the achievement of their individual goals ultimately the organization goal. Thus management tries to maintain high level of morale among the employees. In brief management is attainment of the objectives through harnessing the resources giving equal importance to human and physical resources where the satisfaction of the served and employees will be the prime concern.

Management, organisation, Administration are the three words most commonly used in he management literature. They attribute rather confusing meaning because of he failure t distinguish among fundamental concepts. It is not even uncommon to use these words indiscriminately. Some writers have used management as the most comprehensive term embracing within its scope the entire process of planning policy—making, coordination of activities, maintaining morale and discipline as well as controlling the operations. Some other writers regard all the activities like direction, guidance and control as a part of administration. Certain other writers do not make any distinction between the two. Therefore, it is necessary to define those terms restricting their scope to the field of activity that they designate.

Organisation vs Management

Refers to the mechanism or structure that enables people

to work effectively. In view of George R. Terry "Organisation is the management of functions deemed necessary for attainment of the objective and is an indication of the authority and the responsibility assigned to individuals charged with the execution of the respective functions. In a nut-shell organisation is a basic structure functions. In a nut—shell organisation is a basic structure having established relationships between various factors. It is the task of destinating the departments and the manpower that are to carry the work, defining their function and specifying relations that should exist between various departments and individuals. Organisation is in total a mechanism of management and where management is attainment of the objective through guiding human and physical resources at the utmost satisfaction of those served and those rendering service.

Administration vs. Management

According to Oliver Sheldon "Administration is the function in the industry concerned in the determination of corporate policy the coordination of finance, production and distribution, the settlement of the compass of organisation and the ultimate control of executives." On the other hand management is the execution of policy within the limits set up by the administration for the particular objects set before it.

Breach regards management as an all inclusive function involving responsibility for the effective planning and regulation or guidance of operation of an enterprise. According to Breech: "Management is the total process of executive control and administration is that part of management which is connected with the installation and carrying out of the procedures by which the progress of the activities is regulated and checked against plans".

Fayol and Newman do not make any distinction between the two terms – administration and management. But when the two words are used to indicate deferent functions and not the persons who perform those functions. The distinction assumes much importance.

Taking all these views into account, and on the basis of the generally accepted view e may say that administration means overall determination of policies and major objectives, whereas management is an executive function which is the active, direction human efforts. It is the work that a manager does as he seeks to get results through other people. It may be reiterated that administration as a function is largely determinative and management is essentially executive and organisation in the basic structure that is necessary to carryout these functions.

Management Thought

In the preceding guidelines we examined the writings and contributions of various management pioneers, and saw their ideas evolved through time into one or more aspects of management theory. Every one of them introduced a new fact to the totality of management. Since many of these individuals emphasized different aspects of management and gathered followers through the years, this state of management though following World War II was somewhat a maze. As such, at the present time, management theory is in the School Phase and any author who approaches the field without a basic understanding of these schools will be at a considerable disadvantage. The view points regarding what management is, how it should be studied. Nevertheless the background and training of management theories and practices is reflected in their beliefs about management and in most cases make them candidates for one of the schools of thought that we will be examining in this guideline.

The line of thought adopted here was by reviewing what was done in the past by managers under similar circumstances. By observing what the leading business managers are doing in circumstances similar to ours and applying the same techniques and actions in our managerial work, is what is considered to be traditional approach. Some time, the school is also called as the empirical school, because it contributes generalizations and masses of practical management information. Normally this is written descriptive or in narrative form with the experience gained earlier. This can also be done through a cases study approach or through the study of decision making. The management by customs traditional and also includes the studies of the biographies of outstanding managers and the studies of historians of phenomenal companies. The case study approach helps develop in skill in problem determination and in analytical amenity. It also suggest that if a manager is traced with an actual situation closely resembling the one described and discussed, his best recommendation and solution may well be the one developed for the case study. To this degree, it can be considered to promote use of the custom management.

Management - Science or Art?

Science may be described as a systematic body of knowledge pertaining to an area of study and contains some general truths, explaining past events or phenomena. It may be classified into two groups: (1) Positive science and (ii) Normative Science, the first deals with 'what is and the other with 'what ought to be.

Art refers to the way of doing a specific thing. It indicates how an objective is to be achieved. Art means the 'knowing how', the application. Whereas under science one normally understands the 'knowing why.'

If management is considered as an art, expertise in this field can only be gained by practice. Like any other art, mastering the profession of management requires practice. This practice gives an intuitive knowledge to solve various organizational and managerial problems. Only by experience and practice one gains such knowledge. If management is regarded as science, organisation and managerial problem-requires the knowledge and application of scientific methods and techniques.

Management fails to stand for the tests of either science or art, because management discipline contains both the characteristics of science and art. The science of management provides a body o f principles for law for guidance in the solution of specific management problems and objective evaluation of results. On the other hand, the art of management deals with application of kill and effort for producing desirable results on situations in specific cases.

Art and science of management complement each other and thus. Are not mutually exclusive. With every increase in the knowledge of science, the art is bound to be improved Management art and management science are inter-woven and overlapping in nature. Art of management is an old as human civilization but the science of management is an event of receipt past.

Recently considerable attention has been given to analytical approaches to management resulting in the emergence of mathematical formulate business games, operational research and scientific decision-marking.

Management science is not regarded as exact a science as physics or chemistry, Koontz O 'Donnel and Weihrich commented that management as an inexact science. It is a social science and hence it is subject to certain limitations. The dynamic nature of business situations and he nature of human behaviour are subject to produce uncertainties and to that extent the science or management functions less exactly.

Management as a Profession

A profession has been defined as an occupation in which one professes to have acquired specialized knowledge which is used either in instructing, guiding or advising others. A full-fledged profession usually has the following characteristics:

1. An organized and systematic body of knowledge.
2. A formal method of acquiring knowledge and skill through established institutions.
3. Establishment of professional associations.

4. Growth or professional consults.

5. Professional code and conduct.

6. Licensing to restrict the entry of others, not having the requisite qualifications.

Management profession has almost all the characteristics mentioned above except that it does not require licensing of managers nor it doe restrict the entry of people into this profession, who do not have specialized training. The systematic development or management associations and consultants prove that management is a developing profession. But it cannot be described as a full-fledged profession like medicine or low, unless there is a professional conduct and licensing of managers. Some academicians contend, that the master of business administration degrees should constitute the minimum pre-requisite for entering the profession of management. But per Drucer the father of modern management opposes this idea b stating that "no greater harm could be done to economy or to society than to professionalise management through licensing requirements or specifying special academic degrees as necessary training'. Beside he educational qualification several other factors which influence his performance must be taken into consideration.

Management functions are having he universal applicability. As stated earlier the functions of management viz. planning, organising, staffing directing and controlling are practiced similarly in the organisation irrespective of their basic structure, goals, environment an nature of business. This is known as university of management, it is clear from the fact that management continued its development as an increasingly sophisticated discipline. Today management is accepting the administration challenges of even not for-profit organizations in government, education, charitable, service and healthy-care environment.

In all forms of organisations either profit making or non-profit making the practice of functions of management is one and the same but the technique of performing these functions may differ from organisation to organisation having relation to its basic structure goals, environments and nature of business. Here a distinction should be made between function and technique function is the task that should be accomplished whereas technique is the way of performing that function. Management functions are quite similar in all organisations in the universe despite their diverse characteristics. Hence we can talk about the universality of management. The limitations that organization may select dissimilar techniques to perform these universally accepted functions.

In all forms of enterprises and at all levels of organisation s the environment of management can certainly differ. However, management itself is essentially the same process. The functions apply equally to all the managers., whatever be their level in the organisation or the task they perform.

Management Theory and the Marketing Concept

The relationship between McGregor's Theory Y, concerned with human resources management, and the marketing concept are explored, and some implications of the relationships are examined. The underlying theme of both the marketing and Theory Y concepts is dependence upon participation and cooperation by subordinate units. Both theories need to be extended before widespread endorsement occurs.

One of the most important problems faced by men in all professions is that of "keeping up." For the executive, this means reading in a multiple of areas. Wendell Willkie's One World concept has descended upon business. As interrelationships and interdependencies appear, the scope of the businessman's "specially" broadens. To keep up in his reading, the executive must not only read but also develop the criteria for sifting through the volume of materials.

The acquisition of an up-to-date posture is difficult at

best. So time-assuming can this be that the most important questions rarely. How does this report relate to the one read last week? What applications do the new empirical research findings pose for the future? How valid are the assumptions underlying the newer theories?

This article represents an attempt to gain this broader vision. In and first to approach current business topics in such a manner, this writer discusses upon two recent major developments in business-the newer management and marketing theories. The following paragraphs contain a discussion of these theories origanised around four basic questions. What the management and marketing theories that are receiving attention in current literature? What are the similarities of thee theories that suggest more basic trend or characteristic? How is this basic trend identified. What are the implications of this trend for marketing and management operations and therefore for society? Starting with the first question then, the following discussion will attempt to relate these theories and it present possible implications.

The New Management Theory

In 1960, Douglas McGregor of the Massachusetts Institute of Technology presented in book form some ideas that represented the more advanced management thought of the time. In particular, Profession McGregor emphasized the management thought that related to the managing of the human resources of the firm—a topic appearing in more and more academic and professional journals and one which gains international attention daily. In McGregor's words.

This volume is an attempt to substantiate the thesis that the human side enterprise is "all of piece"—that the theoretical assumptions management holds abut controlling its human resources determine the whole character of the enterprise. They determine also the quality of its successive generate of management.

In his book McGregor stated that every managerial act rests on these and that theory and practice are inseparable;

thus, he suggested that the assumptions about human nature and human behaviour (and so also the statements underlying managerial decisions and thus theory) should be clearly delineated and expressed. In short, McGregor contended that the traditional management practice (Theory X) should give way to a contemporary Theory Y. He built his case by analyzing the basis assumptions of both the traditional and the "called for." A brief summary of the major points will provide a common reference point.

Theory X Assumptions

The assumptions about human behaviour are

(1) The average human being has an inherent dislike of work and avoid it if he can.

(2) Because of this human characteristic of dislike of work, most people must be coerced, controlled, directed, threatened with punishment to get them to put forth adequate effort toward the achievement of organizational objectives.

(3) The average human being prefers to be directed, wishes to avoid responsibility, has relatively little ambition, wants security above all.

With these assumptions as a base, McGregor held that traditional methods actually stress direction and control of subordinates since the section and control of operations includes people as well as things. Although this pattern seems to have expressed the management practice of the years, McGregor contended that these practices should change because the basic assumptions of Theory X are in error and also are lacking a validity.

This is a brief summary of some of the characteristics of the traditional theory of management; a review of what McGregor hoped would replace it will follow.

Theory Y Assumptions and Practice

The more appropriate assumptions about man should be

(1) The expenditure of physical and mental effort in work is as natural they or rest.

(2) External control and the threat of punishment are not the only means the being about effort toward organizational objectives. Man will exercise self-direction and self-control in the service of objectives to which he is submitted.

(3) Commitment to objectives is a function of the rewards associated and their achievement.

(4) The average human being learns, under proper conditions not only to except but to seek responsibility.

(5) The capacity to exercise a relatively high degree of imagination, liquidity, and creativity in the solution of organisational problems is likely, not narrowly, distributed in the population.

(6) Under the conditions of modern industrial life, the intellectual potentials of the average human being are only partially utilized.

The central principle which derives from these assumption sis that conditions should be created to encourage subordinates to achieve their goals best by working for the success of the enterprise.

This summary, McGregor believed that the traditional management practice is based upon assumptions about human nature which are consences of a management practice using organizational concepts derived early military and church organisations—authority through direct and control. If management were to change its practices, the proponents of Theory Y say, the truer nature of man would be revealed. This position, of course, gains support from psychology and sociology research. The manager under Theory Y would create positive conditions in a climate wherein the subordinate would see that fulfilling the needs the organization would in turn enable him to fulfill his own personal needs. The subordinate, therefore, would become much more involved in the matters that affect his work behaviour. He would plan, organize direct and maintain self-control overwork that was his responsibility.

This review presents only the highlights of the newer management theory presented by Douglas McGregor—a theory finding widespread acclaim, acceptance, and expression in other articles, in executive development courses, and in graduate and undergraduate curricula.

Now, let us turn to the development of another new theory representing changing thought in the marketing field. At the moment there should be no attempt by the reader to compare the new marketing concept with Theory Y; this discussion will occur later in the article.

The New Marketing Concept

This new theory sounds almost arrive in its simplicity; that is marketing activity should start with the consumer. While the consumer has always been important, he has not always been the key figure in the design and manufacture of the product. In past years, the problem of reducing cost and increasing efficiency have required the major effort of the corporation; however, a new focal point is being discussed. No long can the engineer demand the most attention. The important man on the emerging scene is now the consumer.

In some instances, men have expressed the newer concept as part of the evolutionary process.

Te function of marketing is still growing within the corporate organized and it will continue to grow for some time to come. Business has comes way since the day when most corporations were production-oriented manufacturing companies. The swing to the customer-minded philosophy brought the marketing-oriented manufacturing company into full bloom.

But not all the experts hold the newer marketing theory

to be a evolutionary outgrowth. Much more urgency and change is expressed such persons as Robert . Keith. In his article, "The Marketing Returns Mr. Keith likens the relationship between the new marketing concept and the traditional one to the revolution in science created by Copernicus. "The market is the center of the economic universe in the sun is the center of our universe." A similar picture is expressed by J. Borch, new president of the General Electric Company. "Under marketing, the customer becomes the fulcrum, the pivot point about which the business moves in operating for the balanced best interests of all concerned."

Problems and Criticisms

Not everyone agrees that the benefits just described are the natural extension of participation. The first charge thrown at the participation proponents is that of manipulation. The social scientists, particularly the newer group of behavioural scientists who have worked in industry, have been labeled by Loren Baritz as the "servants of power." The behavioural servants respond to the wishes of their masters, the corporation executives, who have hired them at a salaries far above their meager university earnings to conduct "research studies" that will "uncover the truth Baritz maintain that most of these "findings" are really post facts findings: a company needs data to support some point and data are found. The Harwood studies, for example, which are purposed to exemplify the benefits to be derived from participation, are seen by Baritz as ingenious methods for having the employees "participate" in a management-planning situation so that the goals of the corporation would be better achieved.

Baritz' criticism has been used here to exemplify some thinking an uneasiness about the use of social findings. Actually, one of two possible assumptions must be made before carrying the discussion further. Our assumes that subordinate units can help set objectives in the best interest of the firm or one assumes that they cannot. If the latter position is held then efforts to guide behaviour in the direction of predetermined patterns must be vulnerable to the charge of manipulation. The control of individual behaviour is beset with many problems of ethics. The reader can survey extend his thinking along these lines to see how involved this charge of manipulation can become.

But the other assumption may also hold. Perhaps the majority of the proponents of the newer management and marketing theories sincerely believe that goals and methods advocated by subordinate units will in fact work for the greatest good of the organisation. What then?

If subordinate units in fact were encouraged to make corporate plans and decisions, the mind would immediately turn to difficulties emerging in many direction. How could responsible leadership be encouraged? How could such units handle complex commodities such as defense mechanisms or drugs? Does the consumer know what he wants? These are only some of the pertinent questions. Even though such reflections ensure up multitude of problems, the discussion here will center about a broader area. Perhaps the most serious and far-reaching implication of the participation movement is the subtle impact it would have upon the standards of society.

The Social System

It has been suggested that the pursuit and questioning of implications is important because so many forces in society (management and marketing, in this case) are striving toward the goal of participation. True, not all locations of the business society may completely achieve this end but because of the striving, the question of direction is critical.

If a corporation actually becomes consumer oriented. This transformation does not come overnight but is the day-to-day attempts to have "the customer's wants become the criteria for corporate decision-making." What will happen to society when participation encourages the acceptance of mass values? Can society's goals be achieved when mass values may delay the process of innovation and individual creativity? And as Irvin Kristol suggests, if segments of our nation resists taking on the values of the masses, the government may become the protector or guardian of these segments—consulting in increased bureaucratic organization.

The point is that the very process of placing participation as the goal may erode the forces within this nation that have been balanced basically by our Constitution (the doctrine of checks and balances). The individual's values can be lost to those of the mass. Can minority or individual rights continue to be respected with this greater emphasis upon mass values?

In the same way that followership should be viewed as the countervailing force to leadership, participation should be viewed as the countervailing force to autocratic decision-making, and cooperation the countervailing force to conflict. In more specific terms, the two new theories being discussed contain an emphasis upon participation by subordinate units. In effect, this movement would invest new power in these groups. If the pendulum swings radically to one side, then it would be possible for the new power groups to overbalance the power of the executive organization. To provide an effective and constructive change, then, the new theories must include more specific corollaries relating to limitations extent, and scope.

12

Measurement and the Marketing System of Interdisciplinary Contributions

During this period an academic discipline and a body of marketing research methodologies have emerged. The result has been a deeper understanding of business action and continued progress toward a more rigorous, penetrating, and multi-dimensional discipline of marketing. Marketing has reached a stage in its development where it can profit and theories from other fields. A vast body of material which is potentially useful to marketing management exists in other disciplines. Contributions from these disciplines may add perspectives to the recognized field of marketing by extending concepts, improving analytical tools, and increasing the effectiveness of decision making in marketing. However, caution and empirical evaluation are necessary before accepting the value of particular findings and techniques to marketing.

This article does not treat in depth specific contributions from other disciplines. The ideas are presented to stimulate further research and thinking. More questions are raised about the merits of the interdisciplinary approach than answers given. Such questions concern the relationship of findings within the functional areas of business administration the managerial and educational implications of the probable extension of interdisciplinary activity, and the contributions of an interdisciplinary approach to systems thinking in marketing management. It is hoped that the discussion will stimulate marketers to examine critically the promising areas of related activity and to select the most productive concepts and tools for the study of particular marketing problems. When this is done, valuable ideas will be gleaned from the interdisciplinary focus. As a result, executives will be better able to cope with the increasingly dynamic and intellectually demanding tasks of managing marketing resources.

Interdisciplinary Approach: Definition

The interdisciplinary approach is often considered as including only findings of non-business administration areas. From this narrow and restricted point of view the approach consists largely of the application of social and behavioral science findings to marketing. Such a limited definition, however, results in a misconception.

The interdisciplinary orientation in its broader dimensions includes not only social and behavioural science contributions but also those of the physical sciences and, most important, those of various business administration areas. The contributions of the functional fields of business administration should be regarded as integral components of the interdisciplinary approach. Findings of such subjects as management, cost accounting production, human relations, purchasing, and financial administration significant stimuli to the development of marketing practice and knowledge. Business administration contributions, while not logically separable from those of the behavioural sciences, are currently more important for marketing management than the latter.

The interdisciplinary approach properly includes the application and integration of all findings pertinent to marketing. It embodies a holistic, dynamic approach to marketing thought, concepts, information and techniques. The strength of this approach lies in adding more meaningful perspectives and new dimensions to various marketing concepts, developing improved techniques of solving marketing problems, integrating findings and theories with marketing practice, and developing a more widely applicable and generally useful body of knowledge. The results of application should be a more comprehensive, logically consistent, and useful discipline of marketing.

Interdisciplinary Approach

The interdisciplinary approach and its contributions are not new in many behavioral sciences. Boulding has stated with reference to economic that:

Something which might be called an interdisciplinary movement has been broad for some time. The first signs of this are usually the development of disciplines...In the social sciences, social anthropology is fairly tell established. Economic psychology and economic sociology are just beginning.

To date most of these elements are still just vague ideas and suggestions and they have not been refined and developed into effective marketing concepts and techniques. However,

The accumulating elements for at least a rudimentary theory of marketing are scattered throughout the literature of the social sciences. Many of them are isolated ideas, often little more than flashes of inspiration to the found in longer discussions of entirely different mattes. Some of them are indirect suggestions concerning concepts and methodology that can be derived from the efforts of workers in economic field other than marketing.

Interdisciplinary Approach: Present Status

There has not yet been any great acceptance of a truly interdisciplinary approach to marketing knowledge. Hybrid disciplines involving the study of marketing have not appeared. A step in this direction may be noted in the development of such courses as psychology of advertising and selling, the econoics f advertising, and marketing management. Yet these are far from the stage of maure hybrid disciplines.

Marketing's use of other disciplines to date may best be characterized as multi-disciplinary. Individual marketers have brought specific problems to psychologists, sociologists, anthropologists, social psychologists, and other behavioural scientists, social psychologists, and other behavioural scientists who in many instances were able to find solutions. These specialists, however, study marketing activities from the perspectives of their particular subject-matter areas. One result as been that the needed cross-fertilization of ideas and the integration necessary to obtain more widely applicable generalizations and marketing concepts has not occurred on any large scale.

Two developments may become part of the next breakthrough in the development of marketing science: a blending of various useful disciplines which would result in a truly interdisciplinary focus, and the emergence of hybrid marketing disciplines. Thee developments will contribute to a more rigorous discipline of marketing. The multidisciplinary practice of using social and behavioural science findings in marketing, now in vogue, can be the first stage in the adoption of an integrated interdisciplinary orientation.

The interdisciplinary approach will be judged largely on the basis of to value to marketing managers. The soul-searching and ferment amount marketing men concerning the merits of the inter-disciplinary orientation.

The interdisciplinary approach will be judged largely on the basis of the value to marketing managers. The soul-searching and ferment among marketing men concerning the merits of the interdisciplinary orientation indicate the general interest in the development of a discipline of marketing management:

Marketing management involves the planning, organising, actuating, and controlling of marketing factors to achieve clearly defined market and corporate objectives. It is characterized by the application of the solution of market-related problems.

Prime values of the interdisciplinary approach to marketing management are insights and perspectives which it furnishes about the fundamental elements of marketing problems. It can be useful in helping to understand market change. The comprehension of the dynamics of marketing action and consumer behaviour is essential for more effective decision making by marketing management.

Perhaps the one constant that marketing managers can be certain of during the future is change. A useful perspective on the future rate of change has been presented by Edwin Teller. Teller stated recently that in each century since 1650 man has roughly doubled his knowledge of the world and of mankind in this world. While any such observation is only in approximation, it is suggestive of the enormous accumulation of knowledge that has taken place over the last three hundred yeas. What interests marketing executives, of course, is the likelihood that this rate of change will accelerate. For instance, scholars in several fields have predicted that they will learn as much in their particular fields in the next century as they have in literally hundreds of years of, in some cases, in all previous history. If this accumulation of knowledge occurs, the sources and quality of potential interdisciplinary contributions to marketing will be enhanced greatly. The rate of acceleration of marketing knowledge confronting marketing managers over the next 25 years could then be nearly as great as that of the past century. This would have a tremendous impact upon marketing practice.

New Concepts: A Marketing Need

Managing marketing effort under conditions of increasing range will require new concept and more creative ways of thinking about marketing management problems. New concepts can facilitate the development of marketing and add creative approaches to problem solving. A basic value of integrating behavioural and social science findings in marketing is developing more comprehensive and meaningful bases for understanding marketing activities.

Firms often have difficulty in clarifying their marketing concepts. For instance, basic considerations such as what a product really is and does for consumers is often unclear. In many cases, the product perspective of the term is significantly different from that of the consumer. Firms often tend to conceptualize their products in terms of technical, physical and manufacturing considerations. The more crucial considerations for company operations may be those of consumer perceptions of the want-satisfying characteristics of the product. Marketing management must be concerned with such problems as consumer-product expectations, channel and brand image conveyed and the biological and psychological needs satisfied.

These are not simple problems. Many consumer reactions stem from subconscious motives. Therefore, it is necessary to probe beneath the surface to obtain meaningful information about them. The behavioural sciences may be able to provide keys to some of the answers. They may stimulate the development of more meaningful information.

Many of the topics studied by other disciplines have marketing connotations. Included among the disciplines investigating subjects which can be used to increase the effectiveness of decision making in marketing are: (1) sociology, with its studies of group behaviour, social class, use of leisure time, symbols and images, group characteristics and their influences in consumption; (2) social psychology, as it is concerned with mass communications, attitude measurements, and public opinion; (3) psychology, which deals with motives, product symbols, projective techniques, images, acceptance of new products, advertising appeals and effects of colour; (4) ecology, which has as one of its centers of study the growth and development of cities and suburbs; (5) social anthropology, which investigates social status and social systems; and (6) demography, which is concerned with population trends, predictions and shifts.

Same of the contributions made to marketing theory and practice by psychology and sociology are quit widely recognized. The potential contributions of many other disciplines are generally not as well known. It will be profitable for students of marketing to pursue a broader-gauged and deeper investigation of related subjects than ha been conducted thus far. If this is done, areas worthy of further investigation will be delineated, key concept identified, and interdisciplinary progress will be made at a more rapid rate.

The point of departure and the focus of study differ among the disciplines. Sociologists, anthropologists, or psychologists studying consumers and consumer behaviour use different approaches than marketing scholars. However, here are frequently great similarities between marketing and other disciplines in both methodology and content. Marketing progress can be furthered by studying the similarities among disciplines rather than by emphasizing he differences. Actually, the overlapping of concepts and techniques among various subject-matter areas is an important aspect of the inter-disciplinary approach to the study of marketing.

Students and practitioners who adopt the interdisciplinary approach should gain added insights into the nature and scope of marketing activity A person's concept of marketing is shaped by the knowledge he gain through his own or vicarious experiences. The interdisciplinary orientation adds valuable dimensions to one's marketing experiences. Marketing may be broadened with an increased understanding of related subject-matter areas. An executive sympathetic to the interdisciplinary approach is not likely to view his problems in strictly functional terms or in terms of only one perspective. He will ten to see more clearly the many dimensions of business problems. The interdisciplinary approach, therefore, can foster the development of a wider purview and contribute to the increased professionalization of marketing.

Reciprocal Relationship

The relationship between marketing and other disciplines can be a reciprocal one Marketing is concerned with the study of human action in the market place, the study of the process of exchange and economic transaction and of the interacting efforts and responses of buyers and sellers in the market. This sphere of human action is essential to our economic system and is growing in importance. The field of marketing provides a testing ground on which to verify, modify, and extend the hypotheses which have been described by various behavioral sciences.

In the future, marketing may be a discipline in which an integration occur between the research findings of social and behavioural scientists and business practice. In this process marketing may become a basic source of concepts, hypotheses, and methodologies to be used by other disciplines. If it does so, marketing may aid in developing a general theory of social behaviour and add to the fund of knowledge about man in his environment.

Marketing Management: Behavioural Science Contribution

Specific behavioural science concept to particular problems being faced by marketing management. It illustrates the value of the interdisciplinary approach in extending the frontiers of marketing knowledge and in helping to solve marketing problems. For example, such ideas of communication and information, motivations and behaviour, creativity, problem solving, and decision making have significant implications for effective marketing management. They are being investigated from different vantage points by such disciplines as psychology, sociology, social psychology, anthropology, and political science.

Marketing Management: Behavioural Areas and Concepts

It presents in greater detail selected concepts from

various disciplines that have marketing implications and portrays something of the nature, scope, and variety of interdisciplinary contributions to marketing management. It is evident that several important areas have been omitted from these example, economics. Since marketing a discipline is essentially economic in character, economics has been one of the major contributors to its development. It I interesting to note that economics is itself becoming more interdisciplinary in its orientation. Boulding refers to this significant development and its impact:

> Thus the economist who realizes the strong formal similarity between utility theory and economics and field theory and physics is probably n a better position to learn from the phacist than one who does not. Similarly, a specialist who works with the growth concept—whether the crystallographer, the virologist, the psycologist, the physiologist, the sociologist, or the economist—will be more sensitive to the contributions of other fields if he is aware of the many similarities of the growth process in widely differing empirical fields.

Many of the functional areas of business administration vital to the development of marketing knowledge have also been omitted from the tables. Students of marketing should be well aware of the significant contributions of management, cost accounting, finance, production, human relations, and other business administration subject areas. They should be able to recognize the interdisciplinary activity taking place long business administration subjects. Integrated studies of administration organization, and business research are being pursued by scholars who are incorporating the relevant findings of many business administration subject areas.

Multiple Approach of Behavioural Disciplines

A word of caution concerning the integration of the findings of other disciplines with the findings of marketing might be injected profitably and this juncture. Psychologists, sociologists, anthropologists, and other social and behavioural scientists are not necessarily any more unified in the concepts they hold of their disciplines than are marketers. Complete agreement does not exist among these scientists as to the most promising lines of development for particular aspects of their subject matter areas. For example, consider the important marketing subject area of motivation. Motivation has been studied at considerable length by psychologists and other behavioural scientists. However, rather than any one unified approach emerging, there are at least three major direction followed by psychologists pursuing motivation studies. A number of different approaches may even be suggested by other behavioural scientists.

First, there is the approach of laboratory, or "rat," psychologists, who have tended to focus upon the physiology of psychology. Ten there are clinical psychologists who have centered on the role of certain psychological factors in motivation. This group tends to minimize the biological drives as influencing human motivation and behaviour. The third psychological approach is represented by the Gestalt psychologists, particularly Kurt Lewin and his followers. Of the three this latter approach may have the greatest significance for marketing people in studying human motives and other related questions.

This Gestalt approach is essentially socio-psychological in nature. It streses the thesis that people do react to environmental factors. From the Gestalt viewpoint motivations and behaviour are analyed as a function of the particular person, his inherent drives, and of the immediate environment of which he is a part.

These three different psychological approaches are cited to indicate that in any one discipline a variety of theories and avenues to the understanding of human behaviour may exist. A problem in trying to integrated and utilize behavioural science concepts in marketing management is evaluating and reconciling various theoretical explanations and research results relating to a subject. As a result, the attempt to integrate numerous and often conflicting explanations of behavioural scientists into a practicable solution can become a highly perplexing experience.

Discovery and Application Disciplines

The behavioural sciences do not as yet offer useful concepts or methods for many problems facing marketing management. Bach has stated:

The behavioural sciences as they now stand do not provide a large reservoir of immediately useful analytical concepts and models.

In the study of certain concepts, marketing knowledge may be more fully developed than other disciplines. For example, consider the study of consumer reactions in the market place the process of exchange, and the analysis of various institutions by marketing. However, it is the promise of help from other disciplines in the development of marketing thought, as suggested in the tables, that concerns us in the long run. It would be sheer folly for marketing management to ignore the potential contributions from the application of an interdisciplinary approach merely because this movement is in its primary stages of development.

With regard to the future development of the social sciences themselves, it has been suggested that by 1975 the social sciences will have a considerably enhanced power of accomplishment, and that these sciences will take on the characteristics of a dual grouping of discovery disciplines and application disciplines.

The discovery disciplines will derive their orientation from special or specific subjects of study, and they will strive for the discovery of facts and of regularities in the flux of social events. The application disciplines, in contrast will derive their orientation from specific problems.

It is likely then that marketing people will be particularly interested in applying some of the important findings of the related discovery and application disciplines. It may be that the findings of other discovery disciplines will be adapted, modified, applied, and tested through the methods and techniques used in solving marketing problems. As an application discipline, marketing may then develop and refine various techniques suggested by other application disciplines. Thereby marketing thought and practice will be enhanced and the total knowledge of human behaviour and the development measurement techniques advanced at an accelerated rate.

Measurement and the Marketing System

In addition to the interdisciplinary information listed in marketing practitioners and teachers are aware of the numerous measurement methods that have been developed by various subject-matter areas. Some of these are being applied effectively to solve marketing problems. Included among these measuring devices are tools such as scaling and thinking techniques, personnel tests, various projective techniques, interviewing and questionnaire methods, statistical sampling and measurements, and mathematical models and programming.

Marketing Measurement

Chart 1 shows some of the more promising contributions to measurement in marketing of five related disciplines: sociology, psychology, social psychology, statistics, and operations research. It lists specific measurement techniques from each discipline which have been, or may be, profitably applied to marketing research. These techniques may be useful in solving problems in such marketing areas as advertising, product and price analysis, sales forecasting, and market potentials. They contribute to more precise cardinal and ordinal measurements in marketing and facilitate the planning and control of marketing operations. In many instances the particular tools borrowed from behavioral sciences are adapted and modified by marketing researchers. Through refinements in application, the basic measurement techniques themselves are improved and marketing research thereby contributes to other disciplines. This classification of measurement techniques is not comprehensive nor are the categories mutually exclusive. There are a number of other important contributing subject areas. Many of the techniques could be classified under several of the disciplines cited. In the chart this has been done only in a limited number of cases to avoid much duplication and still indicate the interdisciplinary overlapping of many of the methods of measuring specific aspects of human behaviour.

Marketing Systems

Marketing administrators may be on the verge of a new level of sophistication in understanding marketing's role in the total system of business action. Business managers generally are becoming increasingly interested in the interaction between the components of business enterprise. Forrester has pointed out that business achievement depends on the successful interaction among the flows of information, materials, money, manpower, and capital equipment within the firm. These five subsystems interlock to amplify one another within the total business complex. Thinking in limited functional term may not be adequate for an understanding of th effects of these interactions. It does not allow for anticipated impacts on decisions, policies, organisational forms, and investment choices within the firm.

In many companies the basic problem involves the integration of the functional fields within the field of business administration itself rather than the integration with such disciplines as sociology or psychology. The problem is one of viewing business as an operating system—a while. The impact of marketing, finance, production, or human relations decisions on other aspects of company operations and on the business as a whole must be considered.

Concluding Observations

The greatest long-run contribution of the interdisciplinary approach to the study of managerial marketing may be its influence upon the ways of making about marketing and business problems, rather than its production of new marketing information. Marketing students and practitioners the interdisciplinary approach should gain insights into the nature and scope of marketing management activities. This is because a person's accept of marketing management, or any other subject, depends largely upon the knowledge of the area gained through his own and vicarious experiences.

Not all of the hypotheses, theories, findings, or facts that behavioural sciences have uncovered need be relected in the interdisciplinary concept of marketing management. Many areas of psychology, sociology, social psychology, and anthropology have only a limited relevance for marketing. There are many highly speculative formulations in the newer behavioural science which are not applicable at present. Marketing management cannot and need not take into account all the information and refinements of other disciplines. It should separate and assimilate those findings and concepts which have a direct bring on central marketing problems. By integrating those ideas which are relevant to marketing management, a more insightful approach and holistic perspective will be developed.

The interdisciplinary orientation does not imply that marketing executives and academicians are interested in becoming marketing psychologists or sociologists. Such is not the case. Neither are behvioural scientists willing to give up their professional identification and become marketing men. However, both groups are, or should be, interested in the relevant concept and perspectives developed by other disciplines. Marketers should be sensitive to the development of improvement ways of thinking about the relationship of academic research to business problems. Some marketing men may be wearing an interdisciplinary halo. They may be too prone to believe that social and behavioural sciences have most of the answers to marketing problems. The assumption is that these sciences are developed well beyond the sage of maturity reached by marketing. However, other disciplines do not have ready-made answers to marketing problems. Thee disciplines are also developing their cores of information and generalized theories and seeking solutions to problems concerning human behaviour.

The immediate results of the interdisciplinary approach to marketing will probably not be startling. The findings which are incorporated and integrated into marketing knowledge from other disciplines are more likely to prove to be evolutionary rather than revolutionary. Today the interdisciplinary approach is in vogue. Business administration people generally accept and endorse it. But if marketers wear the interdisciplinary halo too tightly severe academic and practical headaches ay result.

The challenge facing marketers is to develop in detail specific applications of the interdisciplinary approach. This can only be done if the theories, findings, and concepts which appear in other disciplines are investigated to roughly and integrated into marketing thought.

Instead of merely endorsing the interdisciplinary approach and speaking in vague and obscure language about its benefits, marketers must deal more with the specifics and facts. They should consider concrete applications and values of this approach to the functional fields of business and to particular problems in the fields. One purpose of this monograph is to suggest some of these values and applications.

The interdisciplinary approach does not offer marketing a large number of ready-made pertinent facts, principles, and theories which can be applied directly to solve marketing problems or to immediately advance marketing knowledge. A search of the literature of the behavioural sciences and related areas has revealed a paucity of specific marketing materials. But much information with marketing overtones and implications is available. This information has to be further researched, developed, refined, tested, and adapted from a marketing viewpoint.

This situation is not surprising. Behavioural and social scientists do not have the same interests in marketing problems that marketers do. They are not going to perform the fundamental research in marketing or the basic integration which I necessary to utilize the interdisciplinary approach to marketing effectively. This is a challenge which confronts marketing people. It can not be relegated to the areas of responsibility of other disciplines.

Like other disciplines, marketing is going through several distinct developmental stages. These stages include: (a) the evolution of a body of marketing information based on observations, empirical findings, and philosophic speculation; (b) the formulation of currently useful generalization; (c) the delineation of likely hypotheses which can be tested by various disciplines; (d) the division of marketing into specialized subject-matter areas; (e) the specialization of marketing personnel, both practitioners and academicians; and (f) the development and refinement of research methods and techniques.

Like many other disciplines, marketing has reached a stage in its development where significant benefits may accrue from the application of the interdisciplinary approach. It is at a point where problems of interest to it may be profitably investigated and researched in the light of cooperatives findings. If this is done, the effect will be that marketing theory and practice and the research findings form other disciplines will be integrated and will give rise to more general and useful knowledge of marketing behaviour. It is possible that the interdisciplinary movement can influence substantially the type of education offered students to help prepared them for marketing management responsibility. Educators are concerned with preparing men for positions of responsibility in the next ten, twenty, and thirty years. A fundamental problem facing educators is that of coping with the rate of change and its impact on marketing knowledge in the future.

13

Life Style and Consumer Expectations of New Era Markets

Part of the American life style may be referred to as the American Dream. A big difference exists between the American Dream with its expectations and the dreams and expectations of other countries. The gap, however, is narrowing.

The American Dream as a life style concept includes a belief in equality of opportunity to obtain a good standard of living, to acquire status and success in a community through individual initiative, determination, sacrifice and skill. It involves the contradictory concept of equality for all and the rank and status orderings that result in the social ladders so characteristic of the functioning of our complex society. It requires the maintenance of an open society with opportunity for upward economic and social movement and the availability of education which is a root for social achievement, occupational advancement, and higher incomes on a widespread basis. These aspects of the Dream are reflected in our life style.

The consumer, by his decision to buy or not buy a product, holds veto power over the firm's entire marketing and business effort. Many of the elements that influence consumer behaviour and satisfaction are considered in this chapter The structure and organization of the book, the major topics covered in managerial marketing, and the nature of interrelationships among diverse aspects of marketing management. Among the areas discussed are: the systems approach to marketing, marketing management, the role of consumers and consumer behaviour, the managerial functions of marketing, decision strategies and techniques, and the marketing mix. Some new broader dimensions influencing the marketing manager's job are also presented, including recent developments in international marketing and management's increasing concern with the social responsibility of the firm. These marketing developments are receiving increased consideration because their effect on marketing success is now more widely recognized. Marketing as a field of study is generally categorized as being part of the broader field of business administration. However, marketing also involves considerations that extend beyond these boundaries. Marketing decisions are shaped by and influence the external environments of the firm. Marketing, therefore, has social, economic, legal, international, and political dimensions in addition to its managerial focus. Profitable solutions to marketing problems can only be realized if the significance of environmental change on the firm and its customers is recognized. These external forces which affect consumer behaviour and business action must be reflected in marketing policies, plans, programmes, and decisions.

The Environments of Marketing

Marketing managers, by the nature of their problems, are environmentalists. They give attention to the implications of environmental changes for marketing policies and practices. Illustration I shows the external environment in which the systemic functions of marketing are managed. These environments and interactions affect marketing opportunities, customer behaviour and satisfaction, and the degree of success achieved by the business.

In this model, the major external environmental influences on business actions are categorized as: scientific and technological forces; life style and life space forces; ethical, legal, and social forces; and both domestic and international economic and political forces. Each of these forces interacts with the corporate system. Their impact on marketing management is investigated in further chapters.

The marketing manager needs to appreciate the pervasive influence of these forces on consumer attitudes and behaviour. While the activities of any single business cannot appreciably alter any of the external forces, the converse relationship exists—any one force can affect business outcome. Customers react to and help shape their environments, and market opportunities or problems result from changed customer attitudes toward products and services.

Three linkage levels involved in the analysis of marketing systems are shown in the model.

1. Marketing activities are linked through the corporate enterprise system to the various public and private agencies external to the firm. Examples of these agencies, which are not depicted in the model, include: suppliers; advertising firms and media; financial institutions; governmental and private research organisations; federal, state, and local governmental commissions; transportation companies; and the various publics.
2. Linkages exist between marketing and the other business functions that comprise the corporate enterprise system. These other areas are represented by the firm's human, physical, and financial resources, its competitive structure, and its goals. Because the purpose of this model is depiction of a marketing action system, other functional areas of the business have not been explicitly differentiated. Similar models could be constructed for production, finance, and other functions of an enterprise.
3. The systemic functions of marketing are linked to produce an effective marketing-customer satisfactions

mix. Three sub-mixes—product-services, communications, and distribution—are combined to achieve marketing objectives. The objective of the marketing mix is to balance marketing objectives. The objective of the marketing mix is to balance marketing effort with marketing opportunity in order to provide optimal marketing support of stated corporate goals.

The nature of marketing operations within the corporate enterprise system, and emphasizes that corporate goals are achieved by concentrating on defined areas of market opportunity or, more precisely, on customers in particular market segments. Corporate goal setting is recognized today as a complex process for conglomerate, multinational, multi-plant firms. Like the others, Chapter three is future-oriented. One purpose of analyzing the articles in the book is to enable the reader to better understand and ultimately meet the problems consumers will have in the future. For example, understanding of consumer behaviour is increased by studying trends in life style and life space forces. In Chapter three, some of these trends are identified, and their impact on marketing programmes are treated in detail.

Market segmentation provides one way of identifying marketing opportunities that have arisen because of changing life styles. Broad potential markets are broken down into many smaller segments, each with its own tastes, preferences, values, and needs.

The market segmentation concept is the basis of a marketing strategy directed toward consumers with particular life styles and needs. While demographic methods are basic, other criteria for market segmentation are also useful. Examples of newer methods of segmentation analysis include the determination of differences in buyer attitudes, motivations, values, patterns of usage, and aesthetic preferences.

Consumer motivation is a function of the extent to which human needs are satisfied. One theory of human motivation holds that needs are satisfied. One theory of human motivation holds that needs are arranged on a continuum that ranges from basic physiological needs to those of self-actualisation.[2] An appreciable measure of satisfaction of lower needs is a precondition for emergence of higher ones. The marketing manager's task to is to assemble a market offer that promises gratification of at least one level in this hierarchy of needs.

Consumer behaviour is influenced by the life style ad life space force discussed in this book. Many marketing efforts of American business and many of the changes taking place in consumption cannot be understood unless life style trends are considered.

There seems to be an increasing worldwide interest in personal achievement, social goals, and a better way of life. This has been described as the "revolution of rising expectations" and seems to be worldwide. For example, throughout the world there is an upward mobility thrust toward more education and more real income. The above trends are especially evident in the United States. Trends toward home entertainment and family-centered enjoyment are related to increasing discretionary time and mobility. Changes in the geographic distribution of the population are reflected in a redistribution of the labour force and purchasing power.

Tomorrow's customers may have problems that are quite unlike the buying and consumption problems prevalent today. Future consumers will generally be better educated, have greater mobility, possess more discretionary income, and have more time to spend that income. Hopefully, new communication and distribution patterns will lead to increasingly informed decisions and prompt satisfaction of consumer wants.

Decision Making in Marketing

The articles in Chapter four deal with marketing as a prime focus of managerial decision making. Marketing management is becoming increasingly analytical as models and techniques for information gathering and problem solving are developed, and as new marketing applications of existing scientific methods are discovered. Scientific and technological developments are having a continuing impact on the advancement of science in marketing. For example, the computer is exerting a significant influence on such areas as marketing planning, the evaluation of promotional alternatives, and distribution systems. Some authorities see marketing as the great growth area of computer applications in business. The rapid accumulation of new knowledge is resulting in widespread application of mathematical, statistical, economic, psychological, and sociological techniques to marketing problems. These interdisciplinary contributions to marketing promise better understanding of complex consumer needs and of other marketing problems.

Marketing Management Functions

The functions of marketing management identified in the upper center discussed in further chapters. The functions are marketing opportunity assessment, marketing planning and programming, marketing organization and leadership, and evaluating and adjusting marketing effort. The marketing management team must perform these four entrepreneurial functions if the firm is to develop an efficient corporate marketing system in a changing environment.

Marketing opportunity assessment centers on the delineation of actual and potential customers and their wants and needs. Market opportunity exists when a business either possesses or can develop capabilities that enable it to profitably satisfy the wants of potential customers. The business must continually develop marketing strategies that will enable I to cultivate these market opportunities.

Research and development activities of business, government, and educational institutions are resulting in increasing numbers of new consumer and industrial products. Similarly, increased productivity resulting from automation and other forces has resulted in production capacity that enables most manufacturing firms to produce more than they can sell. The mass production capability of American industry is predicated on the discovery of new markets and the expansion of existing ones. This is one of the factors underlying the marketing orientation of American business.

Planning is essential to the organization, operation, and control of a business. Planning also provides a basis for an integrated systems orientation and a coordinated marketing strategy. The development of new products and new markets raises organizational and leadership problems for marketing management. The interaction that occurs between an organisation and its environment illustrates the dynamics of the systems approach and reflects the demands being placed on the marketing organization and its leadership.

Evaluating and adjusting the marketing effort enables the firm to react to changes occurring in the environment. The process of change—and the ability to cope with it –is a major challenge to marketing management. Financial and integrative controls are used to keep the marketing effort keyed to areas of profitable market opportunity.

A marketing mix consists of three sub mixes—the product and service mix, the communications mix, and the distribution mix. The product and services mix is composed of elements that form the set of utilities a customer buys. Examples of utility set contents include the product, price, services, container, brand, label information, conditions of sale, and warranty. A communications mix consists of the firm's efforts to disseminate information about its market offer to the potential byrs. The elements of a communications mix are advertising, sales promotion, personal selling, merchandising, and special sales aids. The distribution mix I formed of two major components—channels of distribution through which goods and titles to goods flow from the firm to the ultimate purchasers, and physical distribution, which is concerned with loading, transporting, storing, and delivering the product.

The marketing manager's responsibility for formulating an effective mix and for putting it into practice does not culminate with the sale of the product or service. He must not neglect the post-transactional ingredients of his marketing mix if the firm's long-range marketing strategy is to be successful.

International Marketing

The external environmental areas of domestic and international economic and political forces. The evolution of international markets is one of the most significant trends in contemporary marketing. Further chapters presents an international view of marketing and the development of the multinational firm.

Many of the forces described in the book are related to the United States market. However, their impact in the United States Portends changes of a similar nature in many countries throughout the world. For example, the knowledge explosion, particularly in science and technology, is influencing nearly all cultures. New marketing opportunities are presented by widespread rising consumption expectations and increased interest in personal achievement and social gains. Political unrest in newly formed nations around the world reflects, at lest in part, dissatisfaction with present living standards. These people want, and intend to obtain for themselves, those goods now enjoyed by consumers in more advanced economies. Similarly, some nations with controlled economies seem to be moving from a production to a partial consumer orientation. The marketing knowledge and ability possessed by multinational firms can aid immensely in the development of balanced economies in both new and changing political-economic systems. Marketing managers must recognize, analyze, and adjust to the marketing systems of each international market. Attempts to improve the efficiency of these marketing systems must be based on a thorough evaluation of the system's socio-political environment.

Marketing plays a key role in the economic growth of

developing countries. To the extent that the socioeconomic growth of a nation is related to the marketing process, marketing can be a critical element in the development process. Marketing is not only an economic tool, but a political and social tool as well. Ultimately, marketing's most important social role may lie in its contribution to the stimulation and facilitation of world peace.

Dimensions of Marketing

Marketing practitioners and academicians realize that various ethical, legal, social, economic, and political forces are becoming increasingly important for marketing Illustration I identifies these forces as major influences on markets. Their effects on marketing thought and action are discussed in this book.

The socioeconomic dimensions of marketing account, in part, for the growing concern of business and marketing leaders with public and private views of social responsibility in business. Te continuing emphasis on the need for businesses to increase their efforts to fulfill their assigned citizenship roles reflects an expanding concept of business' social responsibility.

In order to fully understand marketing's dynamics and the changes in marketing described in this book, students and managers must not only understand problem-solving techniques, they must also understand the theory underlying these techniques and practices. Some developments that influence marketing as a discipline, the interdisciplinary approach to marketing, and the contributions of theory to marketing management are explored in this book.

The articles included in the book were chosen for their contribution to an understanding of managerial marketing. The perspective throughout is that marketing managers must equip themselves to better understand the problems of potential customers and, ultimately, to help customers satisfy their requirements in a manner that meets the needs not only of customer and firm but also of society.

The Marketing Systems

Marketing managers must be environmentalists, for external and internal environmental change is often the dominant factor in marketing decisions. The rate and magnitude of change and its effect on the firm in the form of innovations, flow of new products, and new competitive pressure are fundamental influences on marketing managers who are attempting to match customer needs and wants with corporate capabilities and resources. The external environmental system surrounding the firm; it indicates the basic environmental forces that influence marketing strategy and performance. These forces are classified as: (1) scientific and technological, (2) life style and life space, (3) economic and political, and (4) ethical, legal, and social. Management's skill in meeting and adjusting to these forces is a significant determinant of the firm's profitability and growth. The articles in this chapter discuss the impact of these environmental forces on such important marketing variables as the consumer, corporate planning, and marketing strategy.

As technology and value systems change, new business problems and opportunities are created by a "society in motion." Consumption patterns, for example, are continually modified and altered by life style forces. These changing patterns are exemplified in the higher aspiration levels and goals of consumers. Constantly evolving consumer attitudes toward products and services create a need for new marketing tactics. The study of life style forces contributes to the marketing manager's awareness and understanding of the complexity of consumer behaviour, and ultimately to more efficient marketing by the firm.

Technological change may be the major environmental force for many firms. We live in a period when 90 per cent of all the scientists in the world's history are alive, and the majority of man's store of scientific literature has been published in the last decade. Thus, it is not difficult to appreciate why marketing management must become increasingly aware of technological developments if they are to focus the firm's resources on the needs of to days dynamic markets. Environmental force interact, as indicated to create marketing problems and opportunities. For example, technology and changing life styles can interact to create a major force for change, as Marshall McLuhan has noted in his evaluation of the impact of television and other communications media on society. Developments in communications technology are shrinking distances and time scales, and the scope of marketing and market concepts must be adjusted accordingly.

Marketing problems should be solved and marketing opportunities developed in light of existing political, economic, and institutional forces. Consideration of these forces is contributing to a broader view of the firm's responsibility to society. Public policy decisions have significant effects on marketing decisions. Marketing decisions, in turn, influence public policy. Marketing managers and public policymakers can make a significant contribution to the process of constructive innovation and to society through the integration of private and public objectives. An effective marketing system is essential to economic growth, not only for a developing nation, but also for a mature economy.

Ethical considerations constitute another environmental force acting on the marketing decision maker. Because marketing is a logical focal pint for ethical evaluations of business, marketing managers should integrate ethical values and scientific marketing procedures. Present-day marketing cannot be understood without recognition of both domestic and international economic and political forces. The emergence of multinational enterprises is none development arising from and contributing to such forces. Competitive pressures in the American economy, together wit other environmental forces, create the necessity for a market orientation in which the consumer becomes the focal point of all corporate activity.

Formulation of a marketing strategy requires determination of an optimal customer-satisfactions mix. Marketing resources and procedures are combined with market segmentation factors and focused on customer needs and satisfactions. The degree of success in blending these elements into a workable strategy is determined by management's skills in planning and establishing corporate goals and in the coordinating of marketing management's systemic functions. These functions and their relationships are depicted. Achievement of the fir's goal and marketing objectives depends on customer response to its marketing mix.

Marketing Action and the External Environments

Life style is an important concept for marketers, because marketing is both a product and a determinant of life style. Life style facilitates the understanding, explanation and prediction of consumer behaviour. It also influences economic activity.

Life Style Concepts and Marketing

A general concept, referred to vaguely as "life style," is being used by behavioural scientists, especially sociologists. The precise nature and scope of the concept is not clear. However, in interviews about life style, several behavioural scientists revealed that they understood its general meaning and its significance for research purposes. They were also willing to discuss relevant life-style research projects and to recommend a body of literature that reflected a life-style orientation. They did not, however, define the concept specifically, and none of the recommended literature contained a definition.

The Life Style Concept

What is life style? Life style is a systems concept. It refers to the distinctive or characteristic mode of living, in its aggregative and broadest sense, of a whole society or segment thereof. It is concerned with those unique ingredients or qualities which describe the style of life of some culture or group, and distinguish it from others. It embodies the patterns that develop and emerge from the dynamics of living in a society.

Life style, therefore, is the result of such forces as culture, values, resources, symbols, license, and sanction. From one perspective, the aggregate of consumer purchases, and the manner in which they are consumed, reflect a society's life style.

Following this defining it is logical to speak of the American life style, our family life styles, consumer life styles, the life style of various social strata, and the life style of specific groups in different stages of the life cycle.

In marketing we have been particularly interested in consumer life styles in terms of the way people individualize, and identify themselves as members of various groups, and the resulting patterns of living. For example, we have gathered and analyzed data on consumer incomes, age groups, and expenditure patterns for decades. The goal is not one of assembling statistics for the sake of statistical information. Rather it is one of translating statistical findings about consumers into models of consumer life styles that will permit us to understand and predict various dimensions of consumer behaviour, particularly purchase behaviour.

- A life style hierarchy may be charted consisting of:
- Culture and Society
- Group and Individual
- expectations and Values
- Life Style Pattern and Values
- Purchase Decisions
- Market reaction of Consumers

Life style, therefore, is major behavioural concept for understanding, explaining, and predicting consumer and business behaviour. It is a more generalized concept than existing concepts of consumer behaviour that have been advanced in marketing. Such topics as mobility, leisure, social class, life cycle, status, conformity, mass, and the family as a consuming unit are all part of the life-style fabric. As a result, life-style studies could foster the unification of findings and theories related to consumer behaviour. In fact, life style is a point of interdisciplinary convergence among marketing and such subject-matter areas as sociology, social and cultural anthropology, psychology, demography, and social psychology.

Economists and marketing people seem to have a different perspective on the value of life style concepts and findings. In most economic studies the life style of a society is usually assumed or ignored. It is part of the "state of the art" and "other things being equal," statements. (One striking exception is Veblen who developed such concepts as vicarious consumption and vicarious leisure.)

By contrast, in marketing, life-style of actors are viewed as among the most important forces influencing and shaping economic activity. They are the very focus of a major part of marketing. Foote, for instance, has suggested that in essence marketers are becoming taste counselors. If this is the case, marketing and life style are surely intertwined.

Since ours is a materialistic, acquisitive, thing-minded, abundant economy, marketing becomes one of the cores for understanding life styles. Therefore, marketing is in a position to make significant contribution to a number of life-style oriented disciplines. Moreover, since our life style is being emulated in other parts of the world, such as Europe, Japan and Latin America, a better understanding of our life style may also enhance economic development theory.

Marketing and the Life Style of Abundance

When we think of abundance, we usually perceive of the physical capabilities and potentialities of a society. Abundance, however, is also a result of the culture itself since it stems partly from physical factors and partly from cultural forces. In large measure, our economic abundance results from certain institutions in our society which affect our pattern of living.

Potter maintains that advertising is the institution

identified with abundance, particularly American abundance.[2] However, the institution that is brought into being by abundance without previous emphasis or existence in the same form is the institution of marketing. It is marketing expressed not only in advertising forms, but in such forms as the emphasis upon consumption in our society, marketing research, marketing planning, the marketing concept, new approaches to product development, credit, the management of innovation, the utilization of effective merchandising techniques, and the cultivation of mass markets; that is the institution of abundance.

Ours is a business-dominated society. Hence, business influences our life styles as profoundly as any other force. One of the unique characteristics of American business, however, is the distinctive approach it adopts to marketing. Marketing has reached its most mature form and has had its greatest impact on life styles in the American economy.

Other cultures have made significant contributions to business thought and practice in such areas as business law, ethics, accounting, finance, production systems, and organisation theory. By contrast, marketing progress to date is uniquely attributable to the American life style, and it is being studied and emulated in other parts of the world. Such institutions and techniques as self service, supermarkets, discount houses, marketing research, credit plans, and packaging are spreading part of the American life style in many parts of the world.

In a life-style sense, marketing is an institution of social control. It is an institution of social control in the same sense the school and the home are. It exerts an extensive influence on our life style which I maintain is for the betterment of our social and economic life. Moreover, since marketing is responsible to a very large extent for our standard of living it is impossible to understand our culture fully, and hence our life style, without some comprehension of marketing.

The impact of marketing on our patterns of living,

particularly advertising, has not been ignored. Advertising has been criticized pointedly, Toynbee, for example, writes that if t ere demonstrated to be true "that personal consumption stimulated by advertising is essential for growth and full employment in an economy of abundance...it would also demonstrate to my mind that an economy of abundance is a spiritually unhealthy way of life, and that the sooner we reform it the better... The moral that I draw is that a way of life based on personal consumption, stimulated by advertising, needs change."[2] These are strong indictments of unfavorable marketing influences on our life style and are reinforced by the writings of such people s Warne, Galbraith, and Schlesinger.

When abundance prevails, however, the limitations and constraints upon business and other parts of our life style shift. Potter writes: "The most critical point in the functioning of society shifts from production to consumption...the culture must be reoriented to convert the producer's into a consumer's culture...and the society must be adjusted to a new set of drives and values of which consumption is paramount."[3] this becomes the challenge of marketing in altering life styles in an abundant economy. Marketing becomes an instrument for changing production-oriented value into consumption-oriented norms.

Marketing and Values

Our basic value system determines the nature and significance of various social institutions. These fundamental values, moreover, are not merely the result of the whims of marketers. It is true that we live in a sensate culture, one which stresses sensory enjoyment, materialism and utilitarianism.[4] Consumers desire and can own those items and symbols that are associated wit status, achievement, and accomplishment. Material values have become important. Marketing responds to, and reinforces, such values in our abundant culture, and in so doing appeals to the senses and emphasizes materialism.

The life-style question still to be answered, however, is

one concerning the relative desirability of our life style with such emphases as contrasted with other life styles. Great materialistic stress and accomplishment is not inherently sinful and bad. Moral values are not vitiated as many critics seem to think by substantial material acquisitions. In reality the improvement of material situations can lead to a greater recognition of intrinsic values, the lifting of general tastes, the enhancement of a moral climate and the direction of more attention to the appreciation of art and esthetics.

This I would suggest is occurring today. It has also been the pattern of the past. In history great artistic and cultural advancements are at least accompanied, if not shaped, by periods of flourishing trade and commerce.

The next marketing frontier may well be an inner one—the market of the mind and the personal development of consumers.[5] Marketing in the future may be geared to filling the needs of this inner frontier. One of its roles may be that of encouraging increasing expenditures by consumers, of both dollars and time, to develop themselves intellectually, socially, and morally. This has already been accomplished to a limited degree: witness the increasing demand for classical records, good books, the attendance at symphony concerts, the purchase of good oil paintings through mail order catalogues, and the support for the arts in general. Social critics, while prone to point out the undesirable impact of marketing on our life styles, have neglected to indicate the progress and contributions that have been made.

Life Style and Consumer Expectations

Part of the American life style may be referred to as the American Dream. A big difference exists between the American Dream with its expectations and the dreams and expectations of other countries. The gap, however, is narrowing.

The American Dream as a life style concept includes a belief in equality of opportunity to obtain a good standard of living, to acquire status and success in a community through individual initiative, determination, sacrifice and skill. It involves the contradictory concept of equality for all and the rank and status orderings that result in the social ladders so characteristic of the functioning of our complex society. It requires the maintenance of an open society with opportunity for upward economic and social movement and the availability of education which is a root for social achievement, occupational advancement, and higher incomes on a widespread basis. These aspects of the Dream are reflected in our life style.

In general, American consumers, especially younger consumers, in living out the Dream exude optimism for the future. They feel sure that tomorrow will be better than today. American consumers believe that they can continue to expand their consumption and increase their relative amount of pleasure rather than merely limit desires. They feel sure they can continue increasing the are of purchasing power under their control.

One result of this optimistic outlook is that American consumers see virtue not so much in curbing desires, but rather in realizing oneself by acquiring the necessary goods and symbols. This optimistic life style has a historical root, for a Kraus has pointed out, unlike the European who only hoped that tomorrow would be no worse than today, Americans felt cheated if tomorrow were not better than today.[6] This orientation is supported and reflected in such marketing concepts and techniques as programmed innovation and product development, install-ment credit, advertising, sales promotion and merchandising activities.

Life Style and Change

In our life style we do not accept institutions, techniques, and products as permanent. Our society contains a rich tradition of expecting and anticipating change. This anticipation results from a conscious belief that change are normal, useful, helpful, and good. We seem to accept what appears to be good today and anticipate that it will be superseded by items that are superior tomorrow. The rather trite expression "innovate or perish" has rich meaning for businesses trying to meet the demands of our pattern of life.

Such an attitude is one of the foundations of aggressive marketing. Girod has written that in our culture, "Innovation, change, mobility, and movement are permanent traits," and that, "In stressing the need for innovation, Americans are fighting for the maintenance of this aspect of their way of life for permanency of the one thing to which they are attached."[7]

By contract, some other cultures which are more restrictive in their anticipations do not expect, hope for, or plan for any great change in their environment. They strive to maintain the status quo. In these cultures which are resolute against the suggestion of new ideas, new products, and new processes, marketing tends to play but a minor role.

To date, technological changes have had the greatest effect on our life styles. Changing methods of marketing are, however, very significant. Consider the effect on our life style, and the life style of other cultures, of supermarkets, self-service, discount houses, shopping centers, automatic vending machines, credit plans, new products, packages, and new communications techniques. Such process and service innovations will have an even greater effect in the future.

Consumers, Consumption, and Life Style

In the scheme of our life style, because of a previous production orientation, the relative significance of consumers and consumption as economic determinants has been under-emphasized. The importance of maintaining physical production is, of course, widely recognized. Only limited reference, however, is made to the corresponding necessity of maintaining consumption. The critical nature of consumption in an abundant economy demands that consumption should not be considered as a happenstance activity. We must establish the necessary conditions for consumption to proceed on an adequate and orderly basis.

Until recently, even the relative significance of consumer investment in our economy was greatly under-emphasized. Business investment, which is certainly a most significant factor in influencing business conditions, received almost all the attention. Katona points out, however, that "growth and expansion of the American economy are dependent on consumer investment as well as business investment...business investment and consumer investment are equally important forces which either stimulate or retard the economy."[8]

What must also be recognized is the important fact that consumer investments are not merely the function of increased income. They stem from and reflect life styles.

A distorted picture has been presented of consumers and the purchase and consumption process. Consumers have been portrayed in much of the non-marketing literature as emotional, irrational, union formed beings, manipulated at will through marketing devices. It is held that conformity, followership, waste, ostentation, and meaningless style changes have been foisted upon consumers by marketers. Rokeach points out, however, that marketers have been using the wrong psychological theory. He emphasizes that the theory that consumers are irrational creatures who must be appealed to only on an emotional level is outmoded. Modern psychological theories view man as "not only a rationalizing creature but also a rational creature curious, exploratory and receptive to new ideas."[9]

Competition as Part of Our Life Style

Essentially, competition is directly related to and can be defined only in terms of the culture and nature of the environment that surrounds it. Competition has its fullest meaning in the marketing environment of a consumeristic economy rather than in a controlled, planned, or cooperative environment such as exists in many other countries.

In thinking about competition, however, we tend to be retrospective and do not relate it to current life styles. In interpreting laws and in our economic analysis we often cling to past or previous models of competition and competitive situations. For example, we often conceptualize competition in terms of an emerging industrial society rather than a maturing industrial society, in terms of price competition neglecting convenience and service competition, in terms of an economy of scarcity with relatively low consumer purchasing power rather than an economy of abundance with widespread discretionary purchasing power; in terms of manufacturers and distributors controlling and dominating the market place rather than an economy governed (or at least influenced to a large extent) by customer sovereignty: and in terms of intra-industry competition rather than inter-industry competition.

In particular, there is a misplaced emphasis, stemming from past economic models, on *price* as the key competitive weapon. This does not mean that price competition is no longer important in our mode of living. Certainly it is. It does mean, however, that ours is a competitive situation in which *price obscurity* and not price clarity seems to be the rule and in which other variables including convenience and service are very important.

We seem to take competition for granted as one of the inherent aspects of our life style. J.M. Clark points out, however, that 'There can be no certainly that competition will remain vigorous in American business," and that "The necessary conditions are a fascinating subject for speculation." The necessary and sufficient condition for the existence of keen, vigorous competition, however, is clear.

It is aggressive marketing. Changes in price, advertising, products, and channels of distribution tend to keep things stirred up and prevent competition from lapsing into routine passivity. To a large extend our marketing technology sets us apart from other cultures. It is a motivating force behind our competitive system and characterizes our life style. Marketing in the future must be recognized as a major institution in our way of life as well as a force that can contribute greatly to the influence of international life styles.

Yet analysts of our culture and life styles have virtually ignored marketing. It is often regarded as but a minor type of activity which is not important enough to be investigated. It has been neglected by psychologists, sociologists, social and cultural anthropologists, economists, and historians. It is treated as though it were a side issue in our economic activity, when in essence, it is one of the core or focal points.

REFERENCES

1. David M. Potter, People of Plenty, The University of Chicago Press, Chicago, 1954, p. 167.

2. Toynbee vs. Bernbach: As Advertising Morally Defensible?" *Yale Daily News*, Special Issue, 1963, p. 2.

3. Potter, op. cit., p. 173.

4. See Pitirim A. Sorokin, *The Crisis of Our Age*, New York, E.P. Dutton & Co., Inc., 1946, especially Chapter III.

5. For a discussion of this point see William Lazer & Eugene . Kelley, "Editorial Postscript," *Managerial Marketing: Perspectives & Viewpoints* (rev. ed.; Hotnewood, III.: Richard D. Irwin, Inc., 1963), p. 683.

6. See Michael Kraus, "The United States to 1865," The University of Michigan Press, Ann Harbor, Michigan, 1959.

7. Roger Girod, "Comment on Consumer Reaction to Innovation," In Lincoln H. Clark, ed. *Consumer Behavior, Research on Consumer Reactions*, Harper & Brothers, New York, 1958, p. 10.

8. George Katona, *Michigan Business Review*, July 161, pp. 17-20.

9. *New York Times*, November 7, 1963, p. 60, "Advertising: A Wrong Psychological Limb?"

14

Growth Opportunities for Retail Business in India

Modern Retail is making an assault on India. Over the next few years we are likely to see the most impressive success stories within the worldwise retail industry. We are undoubtedly going to see dramatic failure as well. The opportunity that is represented by the current minimal penetrain of so-called 'organised' retail has created a whirlwing of enthusiasm that the world has perhaps not seen. Certainly there is no-where else were we have seen a headlong rush into retail by conglomerates with no previous experience in the industry. The investments quoted by our largest new players are unprecedented. It may even seem bizarre to the outside world that the highest level of monetary investment in India is pouring into a sector that is not even recognized as an industry.

Achieving success in modern retail is an incredibly complex blending of many key factors. There is an apparent illusion that it is an easy game. The West has learn its' lessons over decades of experimentation, failure and ultimately a few success.

In India we are attempting to squeeze this learning into just a few years. There is no doubt that it is possible—but it will not be as easy as many thing. India is a unique country with a unique set of circumstances. Our consumer is exploding wit aspiration in our newly liberalized environment. His and her demands are outpacing supply in a poor infrastructure environment that is failing in its battle to keep up. A large scale hypermarket in the West might receive eight large container truck deliveries per day, each scanned into inventory with one simple swipe of a barcode. Hypercity in malad will take in up to 250 deliveries per day ranging from pushcarts to 3-wheelers. In most cases the product is not 'ready to sell' and requires some treatment of packaging or even barcoding a large part of the previously mentioned investments in Indian retail are quite rightly into the back end to build an infrastructure that is largely provided for in the West. Managing a return on these massive investments has no Western lesson to help us learn and may take much longer than anticipated.

Sam Walton said famously many years ago that the three most important aspects of retail were; "location, location and location." I believe this has changed in our current society and the three most important factor now are; "location, product and price." Whilst location remain the number one success factor, more choice for the consumer has meant that she is now looking at product and price in a very chose second and third place respectively. On locations, sourcing retail property in Indian right now is a competitive frenzy with many amateur landowners becoming shopping enter developers. Whilst some prices being committed to by retailers are not sustain able, we are also going to see failure of many of the multi-floored malls with poor tenant mix and no anchor with real daily pulling power. The locations that succeed best in the future will either be one-stop estimation of ferings or conveniently located small stores. Either way, daily or weekly repeat footfall for food and grocery purchases are essential. The West has already taught us that falling in the middle somewhere may lead to failure.

A profitable product offering is a finely tuned combination of customer demand, fresh choice in stock position, space, number of sku's, average price point, gross margin, salves mix, creditor days and days of supply. Manipulating a profitable return on inventory investment across these factors, across many thousands of product lines is a modern retailer's most complex task. It is here that newcomers may learn their fastest her that newcomers may learn their fastest lesson. Inventory soaks up cash like a sponge.

Any successful business venture is made by the people employed in it. In retail, this is perhaps most relevant. The large scale investments are going to require hundreds of thousands of new recruits in the next few years. The exciting and complex world of retail represents a wonderful career opportunity for aspirants a wonderful career opportunity for aspirant young entrepreneurs in India. Scaling up as fast as our industry plans to will however require some extraordinary skill from our people. There are none so brave as those who have not yet failed !

Growth of the Retail Industry

In an environment where spending poor is growing fast, there is one sector that has caught the eye of investor sand customers alike. The retail sector, which was till a few years back limited to standalone stores, boutiques and kirana stores, has radically changed its face. Malls, hypermarkets, supermarkets lifestyle stores have gained importance –not only in the metros, but also in tier II and III towns.

The hypermarket format is slated to emerge as a large segment as metro suburbs become swankier hotspot compared to downtown shopping areas. In smaller towns, retail has empowered women to get freedom from the shopkeeper-in law' with new shopping arcades and malls gaining increasing acceptance among the women of these towns.

With about 11 million spare feet of retail space being added last year, the hypermarket and supermarket formats are giving consumers a lot to spend on, especially with existing players such as Pantaloon, Shopper's Stop and the Tata and RPG groups scaling up fast and new players such as the

Birlas and Sunil Mittal pumping in big money into the market. "At an estimated Rs. 12.8 trillion in 2006, India's retailing sector makes up for almost a third of the country's GDP. Food and grocery items account for a whopping 74 per cent of total retail scales, comprising the organized and unorganized seging the organized and unorganized segments," states a Crisil Research report.

Strengthening the case for oganised food retailing, Sudhir Nair, head of Crisil Research, says, "Farmers are estimated to earn around Rs. 1.8 trillion on food grains and fresh grocery at current levels. Assuming this segment shifts entirely to organized retailing and two-thirds of the savings from reduced supply chain inefficiencies are passed on to the farmer, farm incomes could grow by more than 37 per cent to Rs. 2.47 trillion." It is, however, not yet clear how much would be passed on by the players.

Even if the rules of the game are evolving, some basics remain as relevant as ever. "the here essentials of retail branding are innovation, innovation and innovation. You have to take care of the customer, be in contact, provide an emotional benefit and respect his or her individual style. In a people contact business like retail, it's not about the share of wallests, it's people," said Adre Lever more, CEO of Hypercity Retail India, during the Retail Brand 2007 Summit recently organized by the Confederation of Indian Industry in Mumbai.

The modern retailer is essentially looking out for two thigs that will help this industry grow – increased man-power and more space for expansion. This brings us to an important question: who will win the retail race? Will it be the indigenous retailer with his local knowledge, lobbying power and financial resources? Or will global powerhouses such as Wal-Mart learn to adapt and compete here, armed with there international expertise, western allure and sophisticated supply chains? HEMAN Kalbag, principal (consumer industries an retail practice) at AT Kearney, said while sharing perspectives from the report "Growth Opportunities for global Retailers": 'the answer to these questions will be revealed in the next few years, as there is no singe winning formula or 'silver bullet' strategy."

At least till then, this sector will continue to grow at rapid pace.

- India has one retail outlet per 90 people, one of the highest densities in the industry in the world
- India is the 9th largest retail market, with annual sales in the organized segments at Rs 35,000 crore in 2005—and with revenues doubling every year
- Overall revenues, including those of small shops, is expected to grow 5.5% a year to Rs 28,70,000 crore by 2015 at current prices.
- The organized segment is expected to grow faster, at 21.8% to touch Rs. 420,000 crore by 2015.
- Food, groceries and general merchandise, apparel, consumer durables, food services and home improvement are the top categories in the organized segment.

Job Opportunities in this Sector

Here is a refrain often get to hear from those who aren't familiar with the retail industry: "the industry is facing a people crunch," Many facts could be posited to prove the falsity of the statement. First, the industry is growing at over 100 per cent. The Future Group, for one employs over 18,000 people now, and plans to scale this up to 34,000 by June next year. Now take this number as an industry average and multiply it for players such as Reliance and Birla, who are getting aggressive in organized retail, and Bharati, which is yet to launch in the sector. Then you would realize that the refrain in not true.

On the job openings

Another question is often posed: "Do we have the skilled labour for a retail job". My answer would be, "Yes, you do."

This has to down with the skills a required for the most abundant job opportunity in the sector. Most of the openings in the sector are for frontiline shop people. For this, one would basically need about 12-15 years of education. In case of lifestyle stores such as Pantaloon or Shoppers' Stop, one would need to look at graduates.

Retail jobs do not require specialized skills. Whatever skills are required can be taught in 5-6 weeks. Most retailers put freshers though this kind of training before they begin at the job. With organized retail moving into smaller towns, ob opportunities there have increased manifold. In India the neighbourhood store concept is still very strong. So, most retailers look for people familiar with the area. People who handle the frontline also need not be very fluent in English. As long as they comprehend the language, it's fine if they are not very comfortable in communicating in it. So retail provides a sea of opportunities to the non-BPO kinds whose skills in English are just about passable.

The Course Available

When organized retail first started gaining movementum, there were barely any courses that taught the nuances of retailing. But today, graduates can opt for a number of post-graduate and post–HSC courses specific to the industry.

Students can choose from one-year retail programmes in colleges such s KG Somaiya in Mumbai to courses in retail from the Madurai Kamraj University. The latter is a correspondence course that has already enrolled 40,000 students across 125 centres in India. Since the university does not have centres in cities such as Kolhapure and Sangli, students can enroll through the Big Bazaar outlets there. We encourage our undergraduate employees to undertake this 'earn while you learn' programme to upgrade.

The Future group has a tie-up with an NGO in Chandigarh, which works with people from the northeastern part of India to bring them into the main stream. The group has about 150 people who have been employed at different outlets through this channel. Consultants such as Avataar in Chennai also help us to get the right kind of profiles, especially for our hypermarket business where we also employ women who would like to work from home or do a part-time job.

For post-graduates who have just completed an MBA, the profile of a store manager is not only challenging but also a stepping stone for bigger career opportunities. A store manager is what I would like to calla mini CEO', as he or she is in charge of the store. Like a CEO for the whole company, it is the manager who is responsible for how well a store performs. With over 50,000 people being added to the hypermarket and lifestyle formats alone every year, retail is a sure-shot career opportunity not only for graduates and post-graduates looking for a challenging profile with a quick career graph. But also for retired personnel who have still not lost the steam to work.

Bibliography

Arthur D. Hall, "A Methodology for Systems Engineering," (Toronto, Canada: Van Nostrand, 1962).

Bakke, E. Wright, "concept of the Social Orgnization," General Systems, Vo. IV (1959).

Barach, Arnold B. "U.S.A. and Its Economic Future," Twentieth Century Fund Report. New York: Macmillan Co., 1964.

Baumol, William J. Business Behaviour, Value and Growth, New York: Macmillan Co., 1959.

Buss, Perry, *Marketing and the Behavioural Science*, 2nd ed. Boston: Allyn and BCON, Inc., 1967.

Chandler, Alfred D., Jr. Strategy and Structure, Cambridge, Mass.: M.I.T. Press, 1962.

David M. Potter, People of Plenty, The University of Chicago Press, Chicago, 1954.

Ernet. "Discovering the Inner Jones," *Harvard Busines Review*, Vol. XLIII, No. 3 (May-June, 1965).

Eugene J. Kelley and William Lazer (eds.), *Managerial Marketing: Perspectives of Viewpoints*. Homewood, Illinois: Richard D. Irwin, Inc., 1958

Eugene J. Kelley, "The Importance of Convenience in Consumer Purchasing," *Journal of Marketing*, July 1958. (Also reprinted in this book.

Fred J. Borch, "The Marketing Philosophy as a Way of Business Life," *Marketing Series* No. 99, American Management Association, 1957.

Ferrer, Robert, And Wales, Hugh, G. (eds). *Motvation and Market Behavoiur*, Homewood, Illinoois: Richard D. (rwin, Inc., 1958.

Festinger, L. A Theory of Cognitive Dissonaance, Stanford, Calif.: Stanford University Press, 1957.

George Katona, *Michigan Business Review*, July 161.

G. Charres Y. and Nicosia, Francesco M. "Uses of Sociology instudying ConsmptionBehaviour,*Journal of Marketing*, Vol. 28, No. 3 (July, 1964).

Gottman, J. "Megalopolis: The Urbanized Northeastern Seaboard of he U.S., "*Twentieth Century Fund Report*, New York: Macmillan Co., 1961.

Harper W., Jr., and Levy, Sidney J. "New Dimension in Consumer Analysis," *Harvard Business Rview*, Vol. XLI, No. 6 (November-December, 1963).

Herman E. Koenig, "Theory of Modeling Socio-Economic Systems," mimeographed paper. Department of electrical Engineering, Michigan State University.

Herta Herzog, "Behavioural Science Concepts for Analyzing the Consumer, Paper given at theCnference of Marketing Teachers from Pacific Coast States held at the University of California, Berkeley, September 9, 1958.

James G. Drury, "Is Your Problem Overproduction—or Underproduction of Markets?" Printers' Ink, July 5, 1957.

J.L. Henderson, *The Order of Nature* (Cambridge, Mass: Harvard University Press, 1917).

Jay W. Forrester, "Industrial Dynamics," Harvard Business Review, Vol. XXXVI, No. 4 (July-August, 1958).

J.M. Clark, "Competition: Static Models and Dynamic Aspects," *American Economic Review*, Vol. XLV, No. 2, May 1955.

J.W. Forrester, "Industrial Dynamics, a Major Breakthrough for decision makers," *Harvard Business Review*, July-August, 1958

Katona, George, "Rational Behaviour and Economic Behaviour," *Psychological Reveiw*, Vol. LX, No. 5 (September, 1953).

Katona, George, *The Powerful Consumer.* New York: McGraw-Hill Book Co., Inc., 1960.

Kelley, Eugene, J., *Marketing: Strategy and Functions.* Englewood Cliffs, N.J.: Prntice-Hall, Inc., 1965.

Kelley, Eugene J.: Lazo,Hector: Corbin, Arold:and Kahn, Edward. *Marketing Management: An Annotated Biblioraphy*, Chicago: american Mrketing Associiton, 1963.

"Kenneth E. Boulding, "General Systems Theory—The Skeleton of Science," *Management Science*, April, 1956.

Konrad Lorenz, *On Aggression* (New York: Harcourt, Brace & World, Inc., 1966), p. xi.

Krcoman, H.e., andHartley, E.L. "The Learning of Tastes," *Public Opinion Quarterly*, Vol XXIV, No. 4 (Winter, 1960).

Louis Finkelstein in Conference On The American Character, *Bulletin, Center For The Study of Democratic Institutions*, October, 1861.

Malineau, Pierre, "Social Class and Spending Behaviour," *Journal of Marketing*, Vol. 23, No. 2 (October, 1958), pp. 121-30.

Michael Kraus, "The United States to 1865," The University of Michigan Press, Ann Harbor, Michigan, 1959.

M. Francesco, Consumer Decision Processes: Marketign and Advertising Implicaitons, Englewood Cliffs, New Jersey:Prentie-Hall, Inc., 1966.

M. George, L.F., "The Socio-Economic Status of cities and Suburbs," *American Sociological Review*, Vol. XXVIII, No. 1 (February, 1963).

Neal, James U. *Dimension of Consumer Behaviour.* New York: Appleton-Century-Crofts, 1965.

Nelson Foote, "he Anatomy of the Consumer," in Lincoln H. Clark, ed. *Consumer Behaviour, The Dynamics of Consumer Reaction*, New York University Press.

Nelson N. Foote, "The Image of the Consumer in the Year 2000," Proceedings, Thirty-Fifth Annual Boston Conference on distribution, 1963.

O.R. Young, "A Survey of General Systems Theory," *General Systems*, Vol. IX (1984).

Pitirim A. Sorokin, *The Crisis of Our Age*, New York, E.P. Dutton & Co., Inc., 1946, especially Chapter III.

Roger Girod, "Comment on Consumer Reaction to Innovation," In Lincoln H. Clark, ed. *Consumer Behavior, Research on Consumer Reactions*, Harper & Brothers, New York, 1958.

Sidney Schoeffler, "The Social Sciences," *Challenge, August-September*, 1957,

Simonds, Rollin H.: Ball, Richard E.; and Kelley, Eugene J. Business Administration: PROBLEMS And Functions. Boston: Allyn and Bacon, Inc., 1962.

Stafford Beer, "What Has Cybernetics To Do With Operational Research?" *Operational Research Quarterly*, Vol. X, No. 1 (March, 1959).

Tarpley, Lawrence X. "Marketign Resarch and the Behavioural Sciences," Business Topics, Vol. XIII, No. 1 (Winter, 1965).

Toynbee vs. Bernbach: As Advertising Morally Defensible?" *Yale Daily News*, Special Issue, 1963.

Young, O.R. "A Survey of General Systems Theory," *General Systems* Vol. IX (1964.

Wendell r. Smith, "A Rational Approach to Marketing Management Eugene J. Kelley and William Lazer (eds.), *Managerial marketing: Prespectice Viewponts* (rev. ed.,; Homewood, Illinois; Richard D. Irwin, Inc., 1958).

William Lazer & Eugene . Kelley, "Editorial Postscript," *Managerial Marketing: Perspectives & Viewpoints* (rev. ed.; Hotnewood, III.: Richard D. Irwin, Inc., 1963).

William H. Newman and Charles E. Summer, Jr., the process of Management (englewood Cliffs, New Jersey: Prentice-Hall, Inc., 1961